A SIMPLE TWIST OF FATE

ALSO BY ANDY GILL

DON'T THINK TWICE, IT'S ALRIGHT: BOB DYLAN, THE EARLY YEARS
MY BACK PAGES: CLASSIC BOB DYLAN 1962–1969: THE STORIES
BEHIND EVERY SONG

A SIMPLE TWIST OF FATE

BOB DYLAN

AND THE MAKING OF

BLOOD ON THE TRACKS

ANDY GILL & KEVIN ODEGARD

Da Capo Press
A Member of the Perseus Books Group

Designed by Lisa Kreinbrink
Set in 11 point Sabon by The Perseus Books Group

Cataloging-in-Publication data for this book is available from the Library of Congress.

Grateful acknowledgment is made to the following for permission to reprint from previously published material:

"*Blood on the Tracks*: After the Flood" by Jon Landau from *Rolling Stone,* March 13, 1975. © Rolling Stone LLC 1975. All rights reserved. Reprinted by permission.

"Top Critics Track Dylan" by Paul Nelson and Bud Scoppa from *Rolling Stone,* March 13, 1975. © Rolling Stone LLC 1975. All rights reserved. Reprinted by permission.

"Random Notes" by the Editors from *Rolling Stone,* February 13, 1975. © Rolling Stone LLC 1975. All rights reserved. Reprinted by permission.

"The Best Albums of the Last Twenty Years" by the Editors from *Rolling Stone,* August 27, 1987. © Rolling Stone LLC 1975. All rights reserved. Reprinted by permission.

Positively 4th Street: The Life and Times of Joan Baez, Bob Dylan, Mimi Baez Fariña, and Richard Fariña by David Hajdu. © 2001 by David Hajdu. All rights reserved. Reprinted by permission of Farrar, Straus & Giroux, LLC.

First Da Capo Press edition 2004
ISBN 0–306–81231–2

Published by Da Capo Press
A Member of the Perseus Books Group
http://www.dacapopress.com

Da Capo Press books are available at special discounts for bulk purchases in the U.S. by corporations, institutions, and other organizations. For more information, please contact the Special Markets Department at the Perseus Books Group, 11 Cambridge Center, Cambridge, MA 02142, or call (800) 255-1514 or (617) 252-5298, or e-mail specialmarkets@perseusbooks.com.

1 2 3 4 5 6 7 8 9—08 07 06 05 04

THIS BOOK CAME ABOUT DURING a resurgent interest in *Blood on the Tracks* that began as Bob Dylan's sixtieth birthday passed. Fans around the world celebrated Dylan's return to health and form as he won his eighth Grammy Award, a Golden Globe, and an Oscar following the successes of two new albums and his theme song from the motion picture *Wonder Boys,* "Things Have Changed."

Dylan fans in his home state of Minnesota rallied around songwriter-activist Paul Metsa's musical "Million Dollar Bash" for Dylan at the packed downtown club First Avenue, featuring a reunion of the *Blood on the Tracks* Minneapolis studio band.

Jeff Klein, a lifelong rock 'n' roll fan and photographer whose work appears in these pages, died suddenly in 2002, dreaming of the day this book would see the light of day.

This book is for all who believe that for one brief heartbreaking moment, the guitars were in tune, the voice was on the mark, and every song on the album was a fine, polished diamond. Such is the "raging glory" of *Blood on the Tracks*.

This book is dedicated to the memories of Jeffrey Klein and Barbara Perkins Odegard.

CONTENTS

ACKNOWLEDGMENTS

THIS BOOK WOULD NOT HAVE BEEN POSSIBLE without the support given to us by our families, friends, neighbors, and colleagues who helped us on the path to our destination. All of you are very special to us, and we will always owe you our gratitude and appreciation. We would like to thank in particular Gary Diamond, who introduced the authors of the two geographic halves of this story to one another.

Very special thanks to Clinton Heylin, who was kind and generous in allowing us to quote from his Dylan biography, *Behind the Shades;* to David Hajdu for permission to quote from his book *Positively 4th Street;* to Larry Sloman for permission to quote from his tour memoir *On the Road with Bob Dylan;* to John Harris for allowing us to quote from his review of *Hard Rain* in *Q* magazine; and to Howard Sounes for permission to quote from his Dylan biography *Down the Highway.* Jann Wenner and his able staff provided us with everything we requested from *Rolling Stone.* Mr. Wenner's true generosity is sincerely appreciated. If we might also recommend the words of author Paul Williams to anyone interested in Bob Dylan, he will surely take you on a journey of appreciation and discovery, as will Al Aronowitz, who was kind enough to allow us to use material from his splendid website, *The Blacklisted Journalist*. Andy Gill would also like to thank his various editors at *The Independent* newspaper and *Mojo, Word,* and *Uncut* magazines for their patience in enduring stretched deadlines while he was working on this book. Finally, to our agent, Paul Bresnick at Carlisle & Co, and our editor, Ben Schafer at Da Capo Press, a thousand thanks for your patience, hard work, and enthusiasm in helping this project to fruition. To the lovely Linda, Mindy, and our families for putting up with our obsession: Please accept our love and appreciation for all you are to us.

Interviews conducted with every living member of the bands and personnel who recorded *Blood on the Tracks* were conducted with the utmost respect for those who remain among us. To Tony Brown, whose bass rings true through half of *Blood on the Tracks*, we wish you well and thank you for your magical contribution to Dylan's great work. God Bless Paul Griffin, may you rest in peace.

CHAPTER
O N E

BOB DYLAN STOOD AT A ROW OF VENDING machines with his five-year-old son Jakob, feeding loose change into the coffeemaker, selecting the brew he would sip for the next three hours in the studio down the hall. At that moment, the studio door opened and Chris Weber, a local guitar-shop owner who had loaned the singer a rare guitar for the session, came out to tell Dylan the band was ready for him. Bob introduced Jakob to Chris, and the three of them strolled back down the hall to the studio.

As Dylan settled into his position in the vocal booth, Weber stood in the control room clutching his precious guitar, feeling like a fifth wheel. Maybe, if he was really quiet and unobtrusive, nobody would kick him out of the studio, and he would actually get to see the greatest songwriter of his generation in action, close up. But then Dylan peered through the glass of the booth and gave him a puzzled look, and his heart sank. Well, it was worth a try.

"I was just wondering," he asked, more in hope than expectation, "if I could stay and watch the sessions from the control booth?"

"No, man," replied Dylan. "I need you to play guitar on this."

Astonished, Weber left the control room in a daze and joined the band in the studio, where Dylan was about to change the course of his career by spilling his guts to a troubled world living through uncertain times. Times that were equally uncertain for the singer himself, as at that point everything he knew and loved seemed to be in flux. Rarely seen in public for the previous half decade, the world's most reclusive rock star had that year become its biggest concert attraction. He had changed record labels twice in as many years and scored his first U.S. No. 1 album. And his songwriting had recently been transformed by a course of art lessons that had revitalized his jaded muse.

Less agreeably, his marriage was on the rocks.

This personal turmoil would bring forth Dylan's most compelling batch of material in years, a song-cycle of love lost, love found, love made, and love spurned, which would eventually become the most acclaimed album of his entire career. But not just yet. He didn't like the way these songs had been recorded for his much-heralded return to Columbia Records, and he knew changes needed to be made there, too. So here he was, a few days after Christmas 1974, hunkered down in chilly Minneapolis with a group of unsuspecting unknowns, about to try and get it right, the way he heard it in his head. It was a gamble, but one he knew he had to take.

■ ■ ■

After his extraordinary achievements of the '60s, there should have been no doubt about Bob Dylan's position in the rock firmament. After all, he had almost single-handedly dragged pop music through its troubled adolescence to a new maturity. Then in 1966, at the peak of his powers and his popularity, his ferocious, drug-fueled schedule had been brought to an abrupt halt by a motorbike accident near his Woodstock home, resulting in his enforced retreat from public life.

Throughout the psychedelic revolution of the late '60s— a revolution for which he had served as one of the principal prophets—Dylan holed up in Woodstock away from prying eyes, recuperating from his accident and raising a family with his wife. Few of his fans knew at the time that he even had a wife. She was Sara Lownds Dylan, née Shirley Noznisky, a former model and Playboy bunny with whom he had become involved sometime in late 1964, and whom he married in a secret wedding ceremony in a judge's chambers in Mineola, Long Island, on November 22, 1965.

A divorcée friend of Sally Grossman—wife of Dylan's manager, Albert Grossman—Sara was a frequent visitor to the Grossmans' Woodstock home but lived with her young daughter, Maria, in New York's Chelsea Hotel, where Bob took an apartment in order to be close to her. It was Sara, through her work connections at Drew Associates, a film production company, who introduced Bob and his manager to the young cinema verité filmmaker D. A. Pennebaker, who would make the *Don't Look Back* documentary about Dylan's 1965 U.K. tour.

Apart from her great natural beauty, what probably attracted Bob to Sara was her Zen-like equanimity: Unlike most of the women he met, she wasn't out to impress him or interrogate him about his lyrics. An adherent of Eastern mysticism, she possessed a certain ego-less quality that dovetailed neatly with Dylan's more pronounced sense of ambition. Indeed, so self-effacing was she that for a long time their relationship remained a secret even to Dylan's friends, most of whom learned about their marriage several months after it had occurred. Ironically, a few days after the wedding, Bob was asked by Joseph Haas of the *Chicago Daily News* whether he ever hoped to settle down with a wife and children. He replied, "I don't hope to be like anybody. Getting married, having a bunch of kids, I have no hopes for it."

It's perhaps an indication of the depth of his devotion that he conspired to shield Sara from the public eye in a way that didn't apply to his other female friends. Their relationship, it appears, had been conducted along such secretive lines right from the start: Joan Baez's sister, Mimi Fariña, recalled overhearing Dylan making a secret date with another woman—whom she later realized must have been Sara—mere minutes after Baez had departed from a weekend get-together up at Woodstock shortly before Bob's April 1965 U.K. tour. The following year, Warhol Factory "superstar" Edie Sedgwick was shocked to find out that the young pop rebel she had been courting was actually a happily married man.

Short, dark-haired, and sad-eyed, Sara was a native of Delaware, where, according to journalist and Dylan insider

Al Aronowitz, her father, a scrap-metal dealer, had been shot dead in a stickup. She had been married (and divorced) before, to fashion photographer Hans Lownds, who had transformed her into a magazine cover girl, but she had since set about building a new life of her own, moving from modeling to film production at Drew Associates, where filmmakers such as Richard Leacock and D. A. Pennebaker were impressed with her resourcefulness. "She was supposed to be a secretary," marveled Pennebaker, "but she ran the place."

Sara wasn't really a music fan; indeed, the first time Sally Grossman invited her over to catch one of Bob's television appearances, she apparently expected to be watching Bobby Darin. Bob, though, was immediately struck by Sara, telling Al Aronowitz shortly after meeting her that he was going to marry her, enthusing, "She's *strong!*"

"He obviously fell for her," Sally Grossman told David Hajdu, author of the memoir *Positively 4th Street,* "and he didn't like people prying into his family and the things that were really closest to him. If he was really serious about her, she had to be unknown. That was one of our [the Grossmans'] jobs, to help give him that privacy. Look—he just had a taste of a very public relationship [with Joan Baez], and that wasn't working out very well, was it?"

Sara was, claims Aronowitz, "always one of the most queenly women. She ruled with regal radiance and with the power to calm troubled waters. She'd never pull a scene, but when she was really pushed to it, she knew how to do an icy slow burn." David Hajdu describes her as "well read, a good conversationalist and better listener, resourceful, a fast study, and good hearted. She impressed some people as shy and quiet, others as supremely confident; either way, she appeared to do only what she felt needed to be done."

She appears to have been the perfect marital foil for Dylan, posing no threat to his ego and bearing him a string of children in quick succession. Possessed of a quiet but unimposing fortitude, Sara furnished him with a much-needed oasis of calm and sincerity away from the high-octane hurly-burly and habitual deceit of the entertainment industry. He appears to have found her just in time, as the downside of the fast life was beginning to take its toll. Old friends like Richard Fariña, Geno Foreman, and Paul Clayton had died—Fariña in a motorcycle accident, the others through drugs—and several of his own inner circle of friends, like David Blue and Bob Neuwirth, had slipped into drug addiction or alcoholism. Dylan himself had exhibited a fascination with death since his first album and had recently admitted to journalist Robert Shelton, "You know, I can think about death openly. It's nothing to fear. It's nothing sacred. I've seen so many people die." All around Dylan, darkness seemed to be closing in.

It seemed almost inevitable, then, when in July '66 he was badly injured in an accident while out riding his Triumph 500cc on Striebel Road, near his home in Woodstock's Byrdcliffe neighborhood. Dylan had been an avid rider ever since buying his first bike, a Harley 45, as a teenage tearaway back in Hibbing, Minnesota. He was, alas, a terrible driver. "He used to hang on that thing like a sack of flour," recalled Joan Baez of her times out riding with

Bob. "I always had the feeling it was driving him, and if we were lucky we'd lean the right way and the motorcycle would turn the corner. If not, it would be the end of both of us." After the motorbike crash, it was reported that Dylan had broken his neck, and rumors swiftly spread that he was either dead or in a persistent vegetative state—the next worst thing to dead. As it happened, he had merely cracked a vertebra, but he grabbed gratefully at the opportunity to take time out from his schedule to recuperate. All of a sudden, the biggest rock star in the world became its most reclusive, as Dylan shut himself away from the world up in Byrdcliffe. For the next few years, he shunned public contact, settling down to raise a family, paint, and maybe make a little music when the fancy took him.

Al Aronowitz was a frequent visitor to Byrdcliffe, often schlepping the two-and-a-half-hour drive up there from his New Jersey home with the latest films he had borrowed from a movie business chum, or taking his wife and children up for backyard picnics at the Dylans'. Bob, he freely acknowledges, was hardly a model citizen, with a terrible temper and more than his fair share of bad habits, but Sara knew just how to tame his rages when they were directed at Aronowitz.

"Sara always went out of her way to be kind to me," he recalls fondly. "She treated me as if I was a close relative. Whatever predicament we happened to be in, she always knew what to say to turn it into a joke. I worshiped Sara as a goddess who not only could calm the storm but who also could turn Bob into a human being. Bob was never a nicer guy than when he was with Sara. . . . In the years following his motorcycle accident, Bob acted like a romantic cornball when he was with her. More and more, he depended on her advice as if she were his astrologer, his oracle, his seer, his psychic guide. He would rely on her to tell him the best hour and the best day to travel.

"For me, they were the ideal loving couple. They flirted with each other constantly. Their kitchen-talk, table-talk, parlor-talk, and general dialogue impressed me as certainly hipper than any I've ever heard in any soap opera or sitcom. She was always just as hip as he was. Bob and Sara put on an impressive show for me, a drama full of romance and wisecracks and everyday common sense. I felt proud to be the audience."

Another frequent visitor to Byrdcliffe was folksinger Happy Traum, who had known Bob since the early '60s, when as a member of the New World Singers he had often shared stages at Greenwich Village folk clubs such as Gerde's Folk City. In the mid-'60s, Happy and his wife Jane joined the snowballing artistic exodus from New York to Woodstock and met up with Bob again.

"When Jane and I came to Woodstock in the summer of 1966, we became reacquainted with Bob, with whom we had lost touch after his huge pop success," he explains. "By the following summer we had moved there full time and rented a cabin just a short walk from Bob and Sara's home in Byrdcliffe, the historic artist colony that gave Woodstock its initial renown. Bob was recovering from his motorcycle accident, and he was living a quiet country life with his family. We became quite friendly with Bob and Sara, and our kids liked playing with their kids. It was partly the family connection that brought us together, along with our past history and mutual friends from our Village days."

Happy and Bob would play music together, in a relaxed affiliation that would eventually be consummated on record when Bob asked him along to play on some new tracks he was recording for his *Greatest Hits Vol. 2* album. Happy wound up fingerpicking blues guitar on "I Shall Be Released," adding fills and slide licks to "Down in the Flood," and playing banjo and bass—an instrument with which he was almost completely unfamiliar—on "You Ain't Goin' Nowhere." Like Al Aronowitz, he remembers Sara with great affection.

"Sara was lovely," he affirms. "Fairly quiet, very intelligent, with an understated but distinctly funny sense of humor. She and Jane got along very well, and we enjoyed her company. We often had meals together as a family and shared at least two Thanksgiving dinners at their home. Along with a very small circle of other Woodstock friends, many of whom were not musicians, we had fairly normal family contacts with Bob and Sara."

Happy and Jane stayed friendly with Sara after she and Bob parted ways, and she would sometimes drop in to see them when she visited Woodstock. On one such occasion, Happy had recently returned from a summer playing at folk festivals in Europe in a trio alongside future Dylan guitarist Larry Campbell and future Chris Isaak bassist Roly Salley, who had fallen hard for an Irish harpist they had run into several times during the jaunt. Roly was hanging out at Happy's place when a black limousine cruised up the drive and stopped in the yard. Like others before him, he was transfixed by the black-clad beauty (Sara) who disembarked.

"There is a quality that lives in women," enthuses Roly. "It's an elegance that balances all the inelegance in the world. It isn't exactly the trait of an individual but another quality more vast than that. If it was absent . . . it would leave the earth lawless. It creates by inspiring creation. Cynicism has no place anywhere near it. When you see this elegance in form as I was just then . . . you grasp what's unseen in it, too. Aesthetics reveal but barely figure in the realm beyond that.

"I watched her come across the lawn and thought that the places she had stepped ought to somehow be saved for a while at least. She took the seat beside me on the little couch and struck up a conversation as easily as if we'd picked it up from some moment a week earlier. I would say that she was absolutely and unintimidatingly beautiful. She wanted to know about Ireland. I related the whole gold-plated and raging tale and she calmly took it in. Not only that . . . but she understood. That was the thing . . . she understood. I wished we could have talked more because it was a special moment for me. She'd been introduced only as Sara."

■ ■ ■

While domestic bliss in Woodstock was undoubtedly good for Bob Dylan's health and stability, it had a less positive effect on his music, which slipped into an increasingly middle-of-the-road manner. The diffident *John Wesley Harding*, with its spare, quiet arrangements and its enigmatic references to biblical mythology, was an intriguing follow-up to *Blonde on Blonde*—virtually its polar opposite, stylistically—but subsequent albums such as *Nashville Skyline, Self Portrait*, and *New Morning* were flabby, halfhearted affairs that revealed Dylan's new interest in country music, at the time considered hopelessly out-of-date and conservative. In retrospect, *Nashville Skyline* has become acknowledged as the germinal seed from which grew both the original '70s country-rock boom of Poco, The Flying Burrito Brothers, and The Eagles, and the subsequent '90s "Americana" alt. country boom that spawned the likes of Wilco, Lambchop, and The Jayhawks; but at the time it seemed a bizarre aberration, deliberately sailing counter to rock's prevailing winds. *Self Portrait*, which followed soon after, was even more perplexing and was widely vilified by fans and critics alike for its weak-spirited cover versions and halfhearted instrumentals, which rendered folk and rock into muzak.

"Dylan hasn't handled every role with equal skill," noted rock critic (and future manager of Bruce Springsteen) Jon Landau in his *Rolling Stone* review of *Blood on the Tracks*. "He was unconvincing as the happy homeowner. People who criticize that phase of his work never intended to deny him the right to be exactly what he wanted to be. But they reacted to the fact that he couldn't make that experience as real as he could the emotions of anger, pain, hurt, fear, loneliness, aloneness and strength. Like James Dean and Marlon Brando, he was better at playing the rebel than the citizen, the outsider than the insider and the outlaw than the sheriff."

Inevitably, Dylan's self-imposed exile began to chafe on him, and he made an unheralded return to his old Greenwich Village stomping ground in New York, moving into a townhouse at 94 Macdougal Street, and quietly plugging back into the energizing life force of the city. If he thought his years away might have relieved the pressures of his celebrity, he was sadly mistaken. His return from rural reclusion was torpedoed by the attentions of obsessive fans such as self-proclaimed "Dylanologist" A. J. Weberman, who trawled through Bob's garbage in search of evidence to support his theories that Dylan was a Zionist/smack addict/ whatever.

Over the next few years, he purchased other bolt-holes for the family—a beach house on Long Island, a ranch in Arizona—and in 1973 he leased a large house at 21336 Pacific Coast Highway in Malibu, Los Angeles. He already owned a lot on nearby Point Dume, which he had bought in 1971, but it took two years for him to acquire enough adjacent property to build his "Shangri-La" dome home on the site and properly conceal it from public view with landscaping and shrubbery to protect his privacy. Landscaping also played a role in the structures he completed later that year on a farm property he purchased on the Crow River northwest of Minneapolis, Minnesota.

But in spite of his obsessive pursuit of domestic security and privacy for his own family, Bob Dylan's wanderlust (not to mention his lust) was pulling him further apart from Sara. Their paths, so long allied, seemed to be inexorably diverging, and while they still had feelings for each other, they no longer seemed to want the same things out of the relationship. Rock 'n' roll can be brutally tough on marriages, and those that survive invariably involve a degree of compromise on both sides. Bob had staved off the more damaging effects of such a career by effectively retiring from it, making few public appearances, and shunning the usual promotional obligations associated with album releases. But his reemergence alongside his old running buddies, The Band, on the 1974 tour that became the biggest rock 'n' roll undertaking of all time undoubtedly took its toll.

It's impossible to tell whether the marital problems were the result of a gradual disaffection or were abruptly triggered by some transgression on the part of one or the other, but by summer 1974, shortly after the release of his live album *Before the Flood*, the Dylans' separation was being reported in syndicated gossip columns. The reports initially linked Dylan with former Lovin' Spoonful singer John Sebastian's ex-wife, Lorey—a claim swiftly denied by her. More reliably, they also mentioned Ellen Bernstein, a twenty-four-year-old A&R executive for Columbia Records, whom Bob had first met that February while touring with The Band. Invited to a party in Marin County by tour promoter Bill Graham, an old boyfriend of hers, Bernstein told Dylan biographer Clinton Heylin she got tipsy, found herself chatting to Bob, and wound up playing backgammon all night with him.

The tremors from the Dylans' crumbling marriage would ultimately result in the songs that make up *Blood on the Tracks,* the most personal album of Bob Dylan's career, and the one that finally cemented his reputation as the greatest pop artist of his generation. *Blood on the Tracks* is an extraordinary achievement, recognizable now as the last great salvo of small-scale, folksy integrity, before the wave of soulless, technology-based machine music swept back over popular culture in the '80s. By the time it was recorded, the folk-based lyricism that Dylan had bestowed upon the world had become a hugely profitable genre of its own, with singer-songwriters such as Jackson Browne, James Taylor, Carole King, and Joni Mitchell exposing the intimate details of their lives in what became known as the "confessional" style. Dylan had always denied he was a confessional songwriter—correctly, for the most part—but with *Blood on the Tracks* he would outperform all his peers at their own game.

How could he not? Pain pricks an artist into creation, and when it pricks an artist as prolific as Bob Dylan, that pain is inevitably reflected in his work. Save for a prolonged drought during the '90s, Dylan has been a veritable fountain of songs, hundreds of them—and those are only the ones he's bothered to publish. D. A. Pennebaker and others have recalled how Bob would make up songs, one after another, sometimes three at a time, so fast he couldn't stop to write them down and consequently forgot them. This is a fecund, intuitive talent at work, and when pricked by pain, it can't *not* respond.

In Dylan's youth, the response could be heartbreakingly beautiful—as in "Don't Think Twice, It's Alright," the bal-

lad reflecting the waning of his relationship with Suze Rotolo—but it could sometimes be callow, too, as in "Ballad in
Plain D," the grim, spiteful account of his screaming row
with Suze and her sister, Carla. But by the time of *Blood on
the Tracks*, Bob Dylan had grown up, both as a man and as
an artist, and the result is the most moving, bittersweet collection of songs about love and art and pain ever committed
to tape. Songs that tell you everything you need to know
about the Dylans' breakup, but that tell you nothing at all.
The actual facts of their estrangement are refracted here into
vignettes of pain and loss and, ultimately, endurance—the
knowledge that, with time, the pain will numb, and maybe
you will smile again. Someday.

Shortly after the release of *Blood on the Tracks*, Dylan
commented on a radio show hosted by Mary Travers (for-
merly of Peter, Paul & Mary) that he couldn't comprehend
how people could enjoy the album. "It's hard for me to relate to that," he said. "I mean, people enjoying that type of
pain. . . ." But it's not the pain that we enjoy when we listen
to these songs, it's the way he manages to transmute the pain
into such beauty. The songs on *Blood on the Tracks* have a
collective power and emotional logic that shame the ham-
fisted literalism of the many "concept albums" from the
same era. Here, the thread linking the songs together is more
emotional than chronological: He's not telling a story with
these song-stories, he's giving us an emotional X-ray fleshed
out with different faces, places, and specifics, testing out
how the pain might affect his art and, hopefully, the art illu-
minate his pain.

This, of course, is what art does—it takes something intensely personal and explicates it in a manner that resonates with and enriches our universal understanding. And when that understanding is conveyed with the grace and beauty and sheer enjoyment of *Blood on the Tracks*, we can consider ourselves very fortunate indeed. Exactly how fortunate will become clear in the following chapters, which explain how Dylan's inspiration almost foundered at this most crucial watershed of his career, before being redeemed by the most unexpected of interventions.

CHAPTER
TWO

BY 1974, THE DREAM WAS OVER.

The optimistic period of cultural expansion that had begun roughly a decade earlier had ground ignominiously to a
halt as the 1960s drew to a close, soured by the Manson Family murder spree of August 1969 and the killing of Meredith
Hunter a few months later by bikers at the Altamont Festival.

In the wake, a music industry briefly ennobled by the
high moral principles of an idealistic generation slipped back
into its usual condition of decadent cynicism, its untram-
meled hedonism becoming a powerful motor behind the self-
ish era Tom Wolfe fingered as "The Me Decade." The 1970s
became the high-water mark of rock 'n' roll excess, the
decade in which pop musicians, swollen with wealth and
steeled by ruthless managers, recognized the power they
wielded and flaunted it shamelessly. As cocaine inflated the
self-esteem of semiliterate stars, the most ridiculous and
half-baked of notions were indulged in sprawling, quasi-
philosophical concept albums clad in ghastly gatefold
sleeves, and the overblown caterwaulings of redneck boogie

bands were lovingly documented in live double albums of mind-numbing banality.

Backstage, the ethical envelope was stretched to the breaking point by the decadent exploits of touring musicians, while out stage front, increasingly extravagant and costly spectacles separated these self-proclaimed rock gods ever further from the fans with whom they had once shared some tenuous fellowship. A few years before, you could have watched Eric or Elton or Duane or Jimmy from a few yards away in the fevered atmosphere of a small club; by 1975, you were lucky if you could see them at all from Row ZZ, Block 126, let alone admire their dazzling fretwork. This was the dark period between the advent of stadium rock and the development of adequate big-screen technology, so if you weren't sufficiently distracted by the giant flying pig or the hovering UFO or the scale model of Stonehenge, you were doomed to suffer, if not in silence, then at least in something approaching blindness.

It wasn't just rock 'n' roll that had awakened from a dream to find itself stranded in a waking nightmare. The turbulent changes of the '60s had left virtually every cultural assumption open to question, and across all fields of human endeavor, from politics to the arts, the old orthodoxies were being rudely overthrown.

In America, the most immediately significant change came with the retreat from Vietnam, the cease-fire agreed to at the Paris Peace Conference of January 1973 being followed that June by the House of Representatives voting to block all further funding for military activity in Vietnam, Laos, and Cambodia, after which there was little option but to pull out American troops and cede victory to the North Vietnamese Communists. In its seven-year involvement in the region, the United States had suffered 55,337 casualties: only about an eighth of the number of Americans killed in traffic accidents in the same period, but still more than enough to destroy the populace's faith in such a dubious endeavor—and, ultimately, in a dubious president.

In some cases, the overthrowing was direct and brutal. Aided and abetted by the CIA, in September 1973 the right-wing junta of General Augusto Pinochet ruthlessly snatched power from President Salvador Allende's democratically elected Marxist government in Chile. Some five thousand opposition leaders, professors, politicians, and artists were tortured and murdered, including the singer-songwriter Victor Jara, whose hands were cut off to symbolically silence his guitar, before he was shot with others in Santiago's main football stadium.

Across the globe, political disputes degenerated into violent recrimination. In the Middle East, an invasion of Israel by combined Syrian and Egyptian armies in October 1973 ended in utter disarray, with the invading forces rebuffed within the weeklong Yom Kippur War, as it came to be known. Britain was already suffering regular terrorist attacks by the Irish Republican Army, in both Northern Ireland and mainland Britain: By April 1974, the number of people killed since the start of "The Troubles" had reached a thousand, a figure soon swelled by further bombings in London, Guildford, Dublin, and Birmingham. Elsewhere, insurgency and protest were ruthlessly crushed by unsavory regimes in South Africa, Uganda, and the Soviet Union, where high-profile dissidents such as author Aleksandr Solzhenitsyn and scientist Andrei Sakharov were expelled or condemned to internal exile.

Things could not stay as they were in a world slipping increasingly out of balance. By 1974, the global population exceeded four billion, three-quarters of them living in poverty so abject that the slightest tremor brought disaster and death on a colossal scale. In 1973, drought killed more than 100,000 Ethiopians; the following year this disaster was dwarfed by the famine in the Indian subcontinent, which cost 800,000 lives in India and up to 1.5 million in Bangladesh.

It wasn't all doom and gloom, however. Sometimes the era's pervasive mood of change altered things for the better. Australia's racist "White Australia" immigration policy, for instance, was abolished in 1974, and in July of that year the world became a safer, cleaner place to live when American president Richard Nixon and Soviet premier Leonid Brezhnev signed the Nuclear Test Ban Treaty, the first step on the long path to the abandonment of the Cold War. The most immediate effect of the treaty, however, was to reduce the amount of radioactive material being released into the environment as a result of nuclear weapons testing—a measure reflecting the growing ecological concerns of the time.

This was not the only way in which the writing was on the wall for the liberal democracies of the First World. Increasingly, the economic dominance of America and Western Europe was being called into question. The precipitation by Arab oil-producing states of the 1974 fuel crisis sent tremors through the Western economies, signaling the growing economic power of the Gulf states.

In Britain, the effect was cataclysmic. A protracted period spent trying to balance economic growth, welfare provision, and low unemployment finally concluded in the early 1970s with a series of industrial disputes. The most crippling of these, the miners' strike, brought about the imposition of the three-day working week, ultimately toppling the Conservative government of Edward Heath. By then, however, he had ended thirty years of British procrastination and taken the United Kingdom into the EEC—another example of the widespread rethinking characteristic of the era.

America, of course, had the far more entertaining spectacle of the Watergate scandal to occupy its time. Despite his protestations that "your president is not a crook," in July 1974 the Judiciary Committee of the House of Representatives voted twenty-seven to eleven to impeach Richard Nixon for using his position to "delay, impede and obstruct the investigation" into the Watergate burglary, and to "conceal the existence and scope of the unlawful covert activities."

Further articles of impeachment were added later when Nixon refused to surrender the missing White House tapes he had been subpoenaed to provide, a tragicomic episode that brought the phrase "expletive deleted" into the language. The matter was brought to a head when Nixon eventually admitted his involvement in the cover-up. All ten Republican members of the Judiciary Committee reversed their original decision and voted for impeachment. Four days later, on August 9, Nixon resigned. Although bumbling replacement Gerald Ford immediately pardoned him, the damage was done: The American people would from now on regard their leaders more circumspectly than before.

The aftershocks of the Nixon resignation quickly spread out into American society as a whole. If their president was indeed a crook—or, like Ford, appeared a fool—then what kind of moral compass was guiding the country? As revelations appeared about Nixon's secret bombing of Cambodia, and about the vicious Cointelpro campaign waged by the country's intelligence agencies against supposedly "subversive" elements of its own population, faith in government dwindled even further.

These misgivings were reflected in the era's movies, film being the medium that throughout the twentieth century provided the American populace with its most compelling barometer of national attitudes and sensibilities. It doesn't take too much imagination to view disaster movies such as *The Poseidon Adventure, The Towering Inferno,* and *Earthquake*—all released in 1973 or 1974—as symbolic myths about the foundering ship of state, the crumbling edifice of government, or the collapsing social fabric, and paranoid conspiracy thrillers like *The Parallax View* and *Three Days of the Condor* more directly addressed Americans' growing distrust of government institutions, and especially of the culture of secrecy inculcated by the Cold War. Few Westerns—the most mythopoeically potent of film genres—were being made by this point; instead, downbeat, brooding movies such as *Chinatown, Serpico,* and *The Conversation* provided dark musings on venality. Those few Westerns that did appear had a decidedly elegiac cast to them—most notably, of course, Sam Peckinpah's revisionist take on the legend of *Pat Garrett & Billy the Kid*, in which Bob Dylan himself took a typically gnomic, inscrutable role.

The star system was undergoing radical changes, too. The older generation of gung-ho stars epitomized by John Wayne were firmly in decline, their unswerving patriotism viewed in the post-Vietnam era as, at best, naïve or, at worst, quasi-fascist. Their position was usurped on the one hand by rule-bending, vigilante cop characters like Gene Hackman's Popeye Doyle and Clint Eastwood's Dirty Harry—whose endless battles with ineffectual superiors and a corrupt system were a far cry from the noble exploits of detectives in previous eras—and on the other by a new breed of sensitive, liberal protagonists played by the likes of Robert Redford, Warren Beatty, and Paul Newman.

Although a left-leaning political agenda was becoming an acceptable (and profitable) part of Hollywood culture, in music the political commentaries popular in the folk-protest and hippy eras of the '60s had for all intents and purposes withered away, the old orthodoxies overthrown by a cozier, more suburban sensibility. Which is not to suggest that pop music had become completely homogenized by 1974, although it was undergoing a period of widespread radical change. Nineteen seventy-three had seen a stream of significant innovations and record-breaking achievements, not the least of them being Bob Marley & The Wailers' first tentative incursion into transatlantic rock sensibilities with their *Catch a Fire* album, which triggered a wave of interest in Ja-

maican rhythms and recording methods from the likes of
The Rolling Stones, who traveled to Byron Lee's Dynamic
Studio in Kingston to record their *Goat's Head Soup* album,
and Eric Clapton, whose post-Cream, postheroin rehabilita-
tion was completed the following year with his chart-topping cover of Marley's "I Shot the Sheriff."

Mike Oldfield's *Tubular Bells* and Pink Floyd's *Dark Side
of the Moon* brought a new commercial validity to progressive rock, the latter's multiplatinum success establishing the
Floyd as one of the era's biggest stadium draws—though not
yet as successful as Led Zeppelin, who broke The Beatles'
long-standing attendance record (for their 1965 Shea Stadium
concert) when they drew a whopping 56,800 punters to a
show in Tampa, Florida. Almost unnoticed, despite Columbia's industrious hype, Bruce Springsteen's debut album,
Greetings from Asbury Park, NJ, had sneaked out early in
1973, initially selling a mere twenty-five thousand copies—not
great for the putative "New Dylan," but still twenty thousand
more than Dylan's own debut sold on its first release. Meanwhile, annoyed by their figurehead star's defection to David
Geffen's Asylum label, in the same year Columbia issued a
"spoiler" collection of *Self Portrait* outtakes and covers, called
Dylan—still the most reviled item in his entire back catalog.

In the United Kingdom, however, Dylan's appeal remained strong even through the low points of this era, rou-
tinely securing him chart-topping albums and the occasional
hit single. But even there, he was swimming against the tide
of popular taste, U.K. pop being submerged beneath twin
waves of bubblegum pop and glam rock, both of which

prized artifice over authenticity, albeit to different ends. Epitomized by the huge success of such overnight successes as The Bay City Rollers, The Osmonds, and David Cassidy, bubblegum posited a denial of the human spirit as anything other than a purely mechanical response and was thus lapped up by a mostly prepubescent audience, while glam sought solace from the era's grim realities in a delusory flurry of ruffs and flounces, along with an equally delusory notion of decadence.

Started by the likes of David Bowie and Marc Bolan, borderline underground artists who had somehow parlayed their idiosyncratic manner into a commercial niche market, glam was a reaction to the prevailing workshirt-and-denim style of British hippy culture. Because of the notoriously inclement weather, U.K. "heads" had, as the '60s died away, taken to garbing themselves in ex-army greatcoats, perhaps the drabbest clothing ever devised by tailors; in response, the fashion pendulum swung back violently in the opposite direction as the '70s took off, with absurd flights of fantasy, both sartorial and musical.

Within weeks, even diehard rockers like Slade—previously a boots 'n' braces skinhead band—had hoisted themselves up onto ridiculous six-inch platform heels, while the least glamorous of potential stars found their careers boosted by allegiance to the new flamboyance—even when, as in the case of Gary Glitter, they wound up resembling a plump oven-ready turkey trussed up in aluminum foil. Even a relatively straightforward piano balladeer like Elton John plunged into the fray with suitably gay abandon, the undoubted quality of his material and performances allowing him to carry off with aplomb some of the most ludicrous costumes ever to appear onstage. Battle lines were soon drawn up between the older denim hordes, who became the fan base for the '70s heavy metal boom, and the glam kids, who would ultimately spawn punk rock later that decade. Though they scored hits, neither side was really that interested in singles success—by that time, virtually all serious musicians considered themselves album "artists"—and so the singles charts were plagued by a flood of mawkish middle-of-the-road and novelty records like "Seasons in the Sun," "Billy Don't Be a Hero," "Kung-Fu Fighting," "She," "Tie a Yellow Ribbon," and the vacationer's kitsch favorite, "Y Viva España."

None of the era's dominant strains of pop, however, had much connection with the political realities of the time. Heavy metal, glam, prog rock, and bubblegum were all consumed by attempts to escape reality for some idealized fantasy realm of one form or another. Most of the journalistic duties undertaken in the protest era by folk musicians like Pete Seeger, Phil Ochs, and Dylan had by the early '70s been adopted by a new wave of black artists politicized by the civil rights and black power movements. Most notable were the ambitious projects of soul and funk stars such as Marvin Gaye, Curtis Mayfield, and especially Stevie Wonder, who blazed through 1973 with his musical and lyrical genius lubricated by a new level of technical facility, particularly with the emerging synthesizer technology.

For his part, Bob Dylan shrewdly avoided being swayed by any of the shiny (but hollow) new music styles being offered, characteristically retreating instead into a small red notebook, where he annotated his escape from the anarchy and disarray around him. Although his sustained period of reclusion had greatly increased Dylan's mystique, with rare sightings excitedly reported in the music press, his prolonged absence had effectively destroyed his chart profile, which was by 1974 largely restricted to the album charts. Rushing in to fill the vacuum in the intervening years had come a series of singer-songwriters—James Taylor, Jim Croce, Harry Chapin, John Denver, Don McLean, Neil Young, and the newly solo Paul Simon—who proved vastly more successful, commercially, with the folksy storytelling format Dylan had established.

That style proved durable through the early '70s, offering a faint glimmer of folksy integrity amid a swelling sea of MOR pablum and prog/glam fantasy—though, in truth, folk's rootsy authenticity was by then highly questionable, itself being subject to the increasingly sophisticated blandishments of studio technology. Allied to the baroque tendencies of the psychedelic hippy era, this made for some of the least "authentic" folk music ever heard, while the unthreatening nature of most singer-songwriters' attitudes made for some of the least edifying life lessons ever committed to vinyl. Certainly, compared to the vindictive articulacy of Dylan on hits like "Positively 4th Street" and "Like a Rolling Stone," the pantheistic croonings of John Denver offered a deeply sanitized experience indeed: folk music as a kind of travel documentary promoting the great outdoors.

The area in which the singer-songwriter boom *had* proven aesthetically effective, however, was the thorny and sometimes tedious territory of emotional self-analysis, which was at a premium in the "Me Decade." Established by the likes of Joni Mitchell and Leonard Cohen in the late '60s, the "confessional" style had been adopted with varying degrees of impact by such singer–songwriters as Carole King, James Taylor, and the wunderkind Jackson Browne, who penned some of the breakthrough songs of the burgeoning country-rock movement, such as The Eagles' "Take It Easy." In sometimes tortuous, intimate songs, these composers would transmute their own relationships, attitudes, and addictions, as well as their friends' mishaps and suicides, into anthems sung by thousands at their concerts: an aggressively public catharsis of private affairs, very much in keeping with the era's fondness for self-help "training" programs such as EST and Exegesis.

This was the position—and the genre—in which Bob Dylan found himself in 1974, as he attempted to deal with the disruptions affecting his own marriage. It would be impossible to prevent his problems from creeping into his art, but nobody realized how deeply they would stain it. After years of albums in which his personal life and relationships had been strictly off-limits, nobody's business but his own, Bob Dylan was about to set a new benchmark for confessional songwriting, with an album whose personal revelations would remain half-hidden behind a screen of fiction, the truth only occasionally glimpsed amid the welter of characters, allegories, and shifting time scales. It would prove to be a landmark both in popular music and in his own life.

THREE

NINETEEN SEVENTY-THREE WAS NOT a good year for rock 'n' roll marriages.

In October, Elvis and Priscilla Presley's separation was confirmed with a divorce that brought down the final curtain on their six years of marriage. The same month, John Lennon began his temporary estrangement from Yoko Ono. It was as if, having flirted with domesticity for a few years, rock's iconic figures had suddenly tired of the quiet life and begun hankering after the freedoms that had once been their birthright, and that they could see being enjoyed to the utmost by newer stars such as Led Zeppelin.

Elvis slipped with relief back into the clutches of his Memphis Mafia, indulging himself in a free-running nocturnal round of food, pills, girls, and music, while Lennon relocated to Los Angeles for a protracted "lost weekend" of sex, booze, and drugs in the company of buddies like Harry Nilsson and Elton John.

A similar restlessness was afflicting the marriage of Bob and Sara Dylan. Their eight years together had been productive in terms of family, with a brood of five children—including Sara's daughter, Maria, from her previous marriage, whom Bob had adopted—but had proven catastrophic in terms of Bob's reputation and career. Compared with his earlier work, virtually all of the albums produced during his years of domestic reclusion had been substandard in one way or another, reaching their nadir in the shoddy, soulless double album *Self Portrait*, which had been universally reviled by critics and fans alike. "What is this shit?" asked eminent commentator Greil Marcus in *Rolling Stone* magazine, succinctly encapsulating the concerns of millions of Dylan fans who felt a deep sense of betrayal. The lightweight, cozy country music of *Nashville Skyline* had been hard enough to come to terms with, but *this?*

The half-decent *New Morning* had served as a damage limitation exercise, though few were convinced it heralded a new creative dawn, and the ensuing singles "Watching the River Flow" and "George Jackson" and a smattering of new material padding out the *Bob Dylan Greatest Hits Vol. II* double album only served to heighten the impression of Dylan as a once-brimming well of inspiration reduced to a mere trickle.

Leon Russell, who produced the singles, knew differently. The former session pianist with Phil Spector's Wrecking Crew, Russell had become a huge star in his own right as musical director of Joe Cocker's Mad Dogs & Englishmen tour and had taken the opportunity furnished by his current hot status to invite Dylan to record with him at New York's Blue Rock Studio. While there, he took the opportunity to quiz the legend about his songwriting technique.

"I had put a band together for him consisting of Jesse Ed Davis, Jim Keltner, and Carl Radle," explains Russell. "I took 'em up to New York and made some tracks for [Dylan], then he let me watch him as he wrote the songs 'Watching the River Flow' and 'When I Paint My Masterpiece.' That song actually refers to that event: There's a line in there that goes, 'You'll be right there with me when I paint my masterpiece'—he was referring to me watching him write!

"When he first started writing it, he wrote, 'I left Rome and landed in Brussels/With a picture of a tall oak tree by my side'—I think that he thought the changes that I'd played were 'A Tall Oak Tree,' though they were actually 'Rock Of Ages,' which I think 'A Tall Oak Tree' was taken from as well. Anyway, he changed those lines later. But he walked round the studio, writing in a pad, and he allowed me to follow him around and look over his shoulder as he wrote the whole thing. I was really grateful for that.

"With 'Watching the River Flow,' I made the track; it didn't have any words or melody, and he wrote the song and sang it on top of the track. It took him about ten minutes! He really does write like that; he even types like that, most of the time! He's very prolific, he writes tons. He told me one time that when he was singing by himself, he would write four or five songs, sing them that night, and never sing them again."

But although there was no apparent diminution in Dylan's capacity to create, he seemed to have lost some of the impetus, the sheer desire, that spurred the great works of his earlier years. With his Columbia Records contract nearing expiration, he displayed little desire to work on a new album but was also reportedly bored and unengaged during discussions with Warner Brothers over a potential contract. (It's entirely possible that he only agreed to the discussions to try and force Columbia's hand.) With the notable exception of the concert for Bangladesh in August 1971, Dylan made only a few public appearances through 1971 and 1972, mostly unscheduled sit-ins with such friends as John Prine, and seemed more interested in contributing desultory cameos to albums by Steve Goodman, Doug Sahm, and Bette Midler than in working on his own material. He seemed to be treading water, searching for something that might spark his imagination back to life.

He found it late in 1972 when screenwriter Rudy Wurlitzer sent him the script for *Pat Garrett & Billy the Kid,* to ascertain whether Dylan might contribute to the soundtrack. Dylan, who had always harbored a desire to act, saw his chance and took it, flying down to Durango, Mexico, to discuss the possibility of a part in the movie with legendary wild man director Sam Peckinpah. Recognizing the publicity potential of Dylan's involvement, Peckinpah made adjustments to the screenplay to allow for the singer's appearance as Billy the Kid's knife-throwing friend, Alias.

A Peckinpah set is hardly the ideal place for a quiet, reflective woman, and when Sara accompanied Bob to the film shoot later that month in Durango, she found herself surrounded by a crowd of rowdy, boorish drunks high on tequila and testosterone. Thanks largely to Peckinpah's drinking, filming soon fell behind schedule, and the cast and crew were required to work through the holiday season to make up the time. The weather, dirt, and poor leisure facilities made it a thoroughly uncomfortable experience for Sara, and matters weren't helped when two of the children fell ill and had to be taken to Los Angeles for treatment. The couple took a break in January to visit George and Patti Harrison in England before Bob returned—alone—to Mexico to complete filming.

When his scenes were finished, Dylan went to Los Angeles to record the film's soundtrack, renting a home in Malibu for several months, during which time he was seen out and about with friends such as Willie Nelson, David Blue, and Roger McGuinn of The Byrds. Although Dylan's *Pat Garrett & Billy the Kid* soundtrack was basically just a couple of new songs bulked out with bits of incidental music, one of the songs was the elegiac "Knockin' on Heaven's Door," which furnished him with a much-needed hit single and went on to become a much-covered staple of the Dylan canon.

During the summer of 1973, The Band's guitarist, Robbie Robertson (who had also moved to Los Angeles, where he shared a house on Mulholland Drive with film director Martin Scorsese), broached with Bob the subject of a possible Dylan and The Band tour, rehearsals for which were subsequently undertaken at the group's Shangri-La Studio, a converted brothel in Malibu. It had been seven years since the parties had last toured together, during which time Dylan had shown not the slightest inclination to return to live performance other than as a surprise guest at friends' shows or at benefits such as the concert for Bangladesh. Clearly, it was a momentous decision for him, indicative of serious changes in his outlook—as, too, was his decision later that year to forsake his longtime relationship with Columbia and sign with Asylum Records, the singer-songwriter-friendly label launched by fast-rising young music-biz tycoon David Geffen, a fellow Malibu resident.

Stung by his defection, Columbia quickly released the spoiler album *Dylan,* a nondescript collection of cover versions not deemed worthy even of inclusion on *Self Portrait,* the album for which they had originally been recorded. It remains the absolute nadir of Dylan's entire recording career. What must have particularly annoyed Columbia was that Dylan had chosen this juncture to assemble his most substantial set of new material since 1968's *John Wesley Harding,* and they weren't going to get it.

Released in January 1974, in the midst of the huge Before the Flood tour, *Planet Waves* was an immediate success, furnishing Dylan with the first U.S. No. 1 album of his career. In retrospect, it was a flawed work, but at the time it was enough just to hear Bob back with The Band again, and apparently enjoying himself. Apart from the anthemic "Forever Young," the songs were mostly simple, effusive celebrations of love, though the bitter "Dirge," with its opening line "I hate myself for lovin' you and the weakness that it showed," sat somewhat uneasily amid all the hearts and flowers. Still, it couldn't be about his own situation, could it? After all, the same album's "Wedding Song," with its references to "babies one, two, three" and "you were born to be my bride," clearly referred to his wife, Sara, and it was the most fulsome of romantic tributes, with lines guaranteed to melt the hardest of hearts, such as "And if there is eternity I'd love you there again" and "I love you more than life itself, you mean that much to me." What an old softy!

As it turned out, the most significant line in the song was the one admitting "What's lost is lost, we can't regain what went down in the flood," which threw an entirely different light on all the song's other expressions of devotion. Things, it transpired, were far from stable in the Dylans' marriage, and "Wedding Song" can be viewed in retrospect as the singer's desperate attempt to salvage a relationship heading fast toward the rocks—as if mere words might make up for more destructive shortcomings. "Dirge" could also be interpreted as an admission of shame over a momentary infidelity that endangered a much more important, longer-term relationship

Dylan's life, though, was in the process of changing gear again. His 1974 shows with The Band proved to be the most oversubscribed concert tour in history, with over 12 million applicants (more than 7 percent of the entire American populace) vying for the 658,000 available tickets. It was Dylan's first sustained roadwork since 1966, undertaken in a transformed social climate of laissez-faire libertinism, and alongside musicians whose drug and drink habits had grown more extreme in the intervening years. To Sara, it undoubtedly posed a threat to domestic stability, by reacquainting her husband with the dangerous rock 'n' roll lifestyle from which she had rescued him once before. (At least one woman, actress Ruth Tyrangiel, claimed to have begun an affair with Bob during the tour.) To Dylan, the tour may have been undertaken in an attempt to recapture something of the spirit of his youthful endeavors, though he actually hated the grueling experience. In the seven years since his last stretch on the road, touring had been transformed into a huge, impersonal business enterprise, with most of the fun replaced by an increased workload of promotional duties. It was, he later claimed, "the hardest thing I had ever done."

Bob and Sara had sold their house in Woodstock in 1973, and so when the tour ground to its conclusion, they returned to the family's new West Coast home on the Point Dume peninsula near Zuma Beach, a dozen miles north of Los Angeles. Designed by architect David Towbin in consultation with the couple, the house was an elaborate, fantastic structure topped by a Russian-style copper onion dome, with all the fittings, tiles, glasswork, and woodcarvings handcrafted by an army of fifty-six artisans who, according to Howard Sounes's biography, *Down the Highway*, spent two years camped in tents and caravans on the property as they worked. As costs spiraled out of control, the house apparently became a source of friction between Sara, who relished the opportunity to indulge her artistic side, and Bob, who just wanted a bit of privacy again.

By the end of April 1974, Dylan was back in New York, hanging out at his old haunts in Greenwich Village, catching up with old chums like Dave Van Ronk and Phil Ochs, and even, at the latter's behest, giving a somewhat sozzled performance at a Friends of Chile benefit Ochs had organized at the Felt Forum. With Sara remaining on the West Coast, rumors soon began to circulate about the state of their marriage, particularly when he started spending a lot of time with Ellen Bernstein, a young A&R executive at Columbia Records, who was later widely believed to be the subject of the most emotionally upbeat of the *Blood on the Tracks* songs, "You're Gonna Make Me Lonesome When You Go." He also started taking a course of classes given by art teacher Norman Raeben, which would have a (literally) dramatic effect on his songwriting.

The son of the Yiddish writer Sholem Aleichem, Raeben was a Russian immigrant whose own artistic ambitions had been somewhat sidelined by his success as an art teacher. When Dylan started attending his classes on the eleventh floor of Carnegie Hall, Raeben was a seventy-three-year-old with an exotic past, which Dylan further embroidered with characteristic verve: He was, the singer told friends, a former boxer who had roomed in Paris with the seminal modernist painter Chaim Soutine and had known the likes of Picasso and Modigliani intimately—claims subsequently denied by Raeben's widow, Victoria. He did, however, appear to have achieved a kind of guru status among his pupils, wielding his formidable rhetorical gifts with a kill-or-cure indifference to their personal feelings. As each student worked at his or her own easel, Raeben would move from one to another, critiquing each in turn, loudly enough for all to hear.

"He would tell me about myself when I was drawing something," Dylan later told journalist Pete Oppel. "I couldn't paint. I thought I could. I couldn't draw. I don't even remember 90 percent of the stuff he drove into me . . . and it wasn't art or painting. It was a course in something else. I had met magicians, but this guy is more powerful than any magician I've ever met. He looked into you and told you what you were. And he didn't play games about it."

According to one former classmate, Raeben was particularly fond of berating his students, including Dylan, as "idiots" for their inability to understand forms in terms of shadow and light, a principle he tested by requiring them to draw an object after viewing it for only a minute or so: Real perception, he believed, was a matter not just of looking but of *seeing*. Despite his scathing criticisms, the tutor took a paternal interest in his students and even offered Dylan—whose typically scruffy appearance had led the old man to believe he was destitute!—the chance to sleep in the studio, in return for cleaning the place up. Bob, who had long since wearied of the yoke of recognition, was delighted that someone should take an interest in him with no ulterior motive based on his celebrity.

Whether or not Raeben improved Dylan's painterly prowess is a matter of opinion, but he certainly had a radical effect on the singer's songwriting, with which Dylan had been struggling since around the time of his motorbike accident, finding it now took him "a long time to get to do consciously what I used to do unconsciously." This was all too evident from his recent albums, which, with the exception of *John Wesley Harding*, had been meager affairs lyrically, lacking the biting wit and inventive imagery of his mid-'60s work. Raeben, he told journalist Jonathan Cott, had taught him how to "see" again: "He put my mind and my hand and my eye together in a way that allowed me to do consciously what I unconsciously felt."

In particular, Raeben brought Dylan to a more fruitful understanding of time, enabling him to view narrative not in such strictly linear terms, but to telescope past, present, and future together to attain a more powerful, unified focus on the matter at hand. The immediate effect can be heard on *Blood on the Tracks*, most notably in a song like "Tangled Up in Blue," where temporality, location, and viewpoint shift back and forth from verse to verse, rather in the manner of montaged jump cuts in a movie, or in the fiction of Thomas Pynchon and Don DeLillo, allowing him to reveal underlying truths about the song's characters while letting them remain shadowy, secretive figures. (The jump-cut style would be further developed in the artful, dramatic songs Dylan later cowrote with theater director Jacques Levy for his *Desire* album, such as "Hurricane" and "Black Diamond Bay," though time would be much more strictly controlled in them than in the fluid pieces of *Blood on the Tracks*.)

Less happily, the transformative influence of Raeben seems to have driven another wedge between Bob and Sara, as Dylan explained to Pete Oppel: "Needless to say, it changed me. I went home after that and my wife never did understand me ever since that day. That's when our marriage started breaking up. She never knew what I was talking about, what I was thinking about, and I couldn't possibly explain it."

Armed with his newfound songwriting techniques, Dylan retired that summer to his recently purchased eighty-acre farm alongside the Crow River in Minnesota, where he wrote the songs that would make up *Blood on the Tracks* in a little red notebook. Significantly, Sara did not accompany him. However, Ellen Bernstein, the young A&R woman he had met on the 1974 tour, did visit him there.

"I would come up there for long weekends," Bernstein told biographer Clinton Heylin. "This was when all the kids were little, running around like little children. I would cook and we would run around. He was at his best there, at his most comfortable, with his brother's house down the road. He had a painting studio out in the field, and the house was far from fancy, out in the middle of nowhere. He was very relaxed, and that's where and when he was writing *Blood on the Tracks*.

"He would do his writing early in the morning and then kinda materialize around midday, come downstairs, and eventually, during the day, share what he had written. It was in the notebook, but he would play it and ask me what I thought, and it was always different every time; he would just change it and change it and change it. You definitely had this sense of a mind that never stopped."

Some indication of Dylan's ever-restless mind, and of the ways he would let his art incorporate overheard phrases and observations, can be gleaned from his use in "You're Gonna Make Me Lonesome When You Go" of the evocative location Ashtabula, the town in Ohio that Bernstein had revealed was her birthplace.

"To put it in a song is so ridiculous," says Bernstein. "But it was very touching. [He's] a very caring, loving person and lots of fun to be with, so I didn't tend to sit around and analyze what his state of mind was or why he was doing this stuff. I was much more involved in an appreciation of knowing someone who had that kind of ability to express himself and how interesting it was to see it in process and be part of that process.

"I think he's always in some measure of pain, being that creative. That kind of artistic genius goes hand-in-hand with demons. . . . [But then] I think he is generally uncomfortable in his own skin. [And yet] when he was on the farm, nobody was around [who] was looking at him, or wanting from him; it was just me and the kids and his brother, in a state where he felt comfortable, with his paints and his guitar and some food. He would get so excited by my homemade granola. I think I sewed him a black vest while I was there, and he just thought that was fantastic!"

Apart from the obvious attractions of dating—albeit secretly—a legendary rock star, for Bernstein the liaison appears to have offered the opportunity to sample a taste of rural domestic bliss without the obligations of commitment. But beneath the contented surface of the situation, her very presence there begged certain questions about the state of the Dylans' marriage—questions that remained firmly unbroached by both sides.

"I felt sorta like 'Don't ask, don't tell,'" recalls Bernstein. "I was a very young twenty-four. I was not terribly sophisticated. This was brand-new stuff to me, so I never thought to ask, 'So, what's going on with your wife?' I didn't want to get married, and I wasn't being asked to leave."

Before the summer was through, Dylan's red notebook contained seventeen completed songs, ten of which would make up *Blood on the Tracks*. According to Ellen Bernstein, by then Bob already had a pretty shrewd idea which ten they would be. "I think, as he wrote the songs, and as he played them for people, the sequencing decided itself," she believes. "He really was definite when he went in; he knew what he was going to do, and he knew how he was going to do it."

By July, Bob was excitedly playing the new songs for friends like Crosby, Stills & Nash, Tim Drummond, Peter Rowan, and Mike Bloomfield, while behind the scenes his representatives hammered out the details of his imminent return to Columbia Records.

Stephen Stills, for one, was not impressed with Dylan's new material. On July 22, 1974, at the St. Paul Hilton, according to Graham Nash, "Dylan comes to the hotel. [Tim] Drummond and Stephen commandeer him and won't let anybody else in the room." Dylan picked up an acoustic guitar and proceeded to play most of his new material for *Blood on the Tracks,* while Nash stood at the door eavesdropping. "I'm listening to these songs through the door," recalled Nash. "I'm fucking *dying.*" The moment Dylan left, claims Nash, "Stephen looks at me—and this is a direct quote—he said, 'He's no musician.' I said, '*What?*' 'He's a good songwriter . . . but he's no musician'!"

By early August, Bob was staying at Ellen Bernstein's home in Oakland, California. He was eager to try out his new material for friends and paid a secretive visit to the Marin County home of Michael Bloomfield, an alumnus of his earlier masterpiece, *Highway 61 Revisited.* On that classic Dylan album, Bloomfield had recorded the soaring guitar leads, which jump out from the mix in Dylan's break-through single, "Like a Rolling Stone." This time Bob, in his unbridled enthusiasm, chose to steamroller through the material in an open D tuning, without pause, giving his old friend no time to grasp or learn the material.

"It was very uncomfortable with Bob and very intimidating," Bloomfield told celebrated rock journalist Larry "Ratso" Sloman. "You know how Bob sort of taps his foot, man, like that very hyper foot tapping away, it makes you very uncomfortable, like 'Let's get on with it.' But get on with what? All it would take was a little time, enough time to say, 'Hey, Bob, listen, one song at a time, let me learn it, and when I know it I know it and it's done.'

"He took out his guitar, tuned to open D tuning and started playing the songs nonstop! And he just played them all and I sort of picked along with it . . . but he was selling the whole song, and they weren't short songs. . . . I was saying, 'No man, don't sing the whole thing, just one chorus and . . . let me write it down so I can play with you.' And he didn't. He just kept on playing one after another and I got lost; they all began to sound the same to me, they were all in the same key, they were all long. I don't know; it was one of the strangest experiences of my life. And it really hurt me.

"I just felt this big wall, this enormous barrier that was so tangible that there was no way you could say, 'Hey man, how are you? Drinking a lot still? How are your kids?' because anything like that would seem like ass-kissing or an invasion of his privacy. It just made me feel very uncomfortable."

This was not the last time Mike Bloomfield would meet Bob Dylan; on November 15, 1980, he joined Bob onstage at the Warfield Theater in San Francisco and jammed on "Like a Rolling Stone," the song they had recorded together fifteen years earlier. Tragically, Bloomfield was found dead in his car of a drug overdose in San Francisco on February 15, 1981.

Dylan would get a much more positive reaction than that offered by Stills and Bloomfield when Ellen Bernstein took the opportunity to introduce him to Shel Silverstein, the noted children's poet and cartoonist and one of Bob's favorite country composers, whose songs had provided the biggest hits of their careers for such charting artists as Dr. Hook ("Sylvia's Mother") and Johnny Cash ("A Boy Named Sue"). Their visit to Silverstein's fairly luxurious houseboat culminated in Bob's sitting down and playing him "every song on *Blood on the Tracks*, every single one, and Shel loved it."

Encouraged, Bob set about preparing to record the new material, which would comprise the first album of the new contract he had signed with Columbia on August 1, 1974— much to the disgruntlement of David Geffen, who probably suspected that Dylan had simply used his temporary affiliation with Geffen's Asylum Records as leverage to improve his deal with Columbia. "Bob Dylan has made a decision to bet on his past," Geffen noted sardonically. As things turned out, it would be a bet that paid off handsomely for the resurgent legend.

INTERLUDE

ON AUGUST 8, 1974, JUST AS BOB DYLAN was readying himself
to record one of the landmark albums of his career, the resignation of President Richard Nixon sent shockwaves across
the nation. As with the assassination of John F. Kennedy, few
would forget where they were when they learned the news.

Up in Kasota, Minnesota, a part-time guitarist and
Chicago & Northwestern Railroad brakeman called Kevin
Odegard stood on the rear platform of a caboose parked in
a siding, waiting for a hot northbound train to pass by.

"It was the Viking Fruit Express," he recalls, "and everyone just got out of the way when it was coming because it
was a huge moneymaker for the C&NW, packed with per-
ishable produce."

As the train approached a grain elevator near the parked
diesel locomotive, a large chunk of cinder blew out of the
stack of the speeding Viking Express, caught the breeze, and
blew into the grain elevator.

"The dust in there just ignited and blew up the place, top
to bottom, in a matter of minutes," marvels Odegard. "The

main line heated up and bowed out away from the flames, so we could go no further. They sent a taxi for our crew and brought us down to the Boston Hotel in St. James, Minnesota, where we sat sipping brandy, watching the videotape of Nixon resigning, over and over, until we all just drifted off to our rooms and slept it off."

The news was welcomed by most right-thinking—as opposed to right-leaning—people, including banjo player Eric Weissberg, whose band Deliverance was still enjoying a healthy workload on the back of Weissberg and Steve Mandell's "Dueling Banjos," a massive worldwide hit single the previous year.

"Nixon was a schmuck and a creep," believes Weissberg to this day. "He got what he should have."

Deliverance drummer Richard Crooks remembers feeling a pang of pity for the fallen politician.

"At the time, I felt bad for the guy, because he got caught," he recalls. "Everybody else in that office, especially since then, has done something, and prior to that there was always something shady going down behind those closed doors. But he just got caught, and unfortunately he didn't handle it that well, trying to cover it up. He couldn't come out and say, 'Okay, I was a part of this thing,' because a lot of other people would have gone down with him—because the president is just the president, and the machine is this huge underpinning of which we know so little."

In Minneapolis, a Dylan landmark was changing hands in 1974, just as Nixon resigned. A young entrepreneurial couple, Chris and Vanessa Weber, were closing on their purchase of The Podium, the Twin Cities' most respected guitar shop, in the Dinkytown campus neighborhood, which had experienced considerable student unrest following the invasion of Cambodia, when the University of Minnesota had been shut down entirely. They had been managing and building up the clientele at The Podium for nearly five years. Little did they realize how their new purchase would soon bring the store back in contact with Bob Dylan.

"Like many others, I hated Nixon," says Chris Weber. "There was a little bit of concern at the time because here we were, pregnant with our first child, purchasing a music store, putting our life on the line for a whole lot of money, and we had no idea how this political situation was going to affect the campus, financially, because of the effect it had on the whole student population—there was jubilation in Dinkytown, and 'Revolution in the Air!' Here we were, buried in the heart of this revolutionary store that sold everything from guitars to paraphernalia, and we're doing inventory on this merchandise and wondering how this was going to balance with our sense of rebellion.

"Suddenly, we had one foot on Republican turf and one foot on Democrat turf, so we were nervous. We were heavily patronized by the 'revolutionaries,' the players who interpreted what was happening on campus, standing on street corners busking for coins, or playing at the Whole Coffeehouse or the New Riverside Café. The street performers were constantly coming in our store saying, 'Isn't it wonderful!' and 'Isn't it great!' and we're thinking, 'Well, yeah, it's wonderful, but how's it going to expose us?'"

A little way across town, Billy Petersen, Minneapolis's most talented and prolific bass player, was gigging six nights a week with the jazz group Natural Life at The Longhorn in the Lumber Exchange Building at Fourth and Hennepin. "It was owned by the Blumenthals," he recalls, "and they always loved the cats [musicians] and treated us well. Our first drummer had left the group by this time and packed his car to move to LA, but we were serious about keeping the Longhorn gig and getting a recording deal."

Bill Berg, Natural Life's newly departed drummer, had been stationed in Guam with the U.S. Navy when President Nixon had visited the island in 1969. As Nixon stumbled off the plane, Berg and the rest of the military band broke into "Hail to the Chief."

"I played the type of military snare drum that hung around your neck on a rope, so you could march along and play it at the same time," explains Berg. "I guess that style of drumming helped adapt me for any situation that came my way later on, when I started doing studio dates. The next time I remember seeing Nixon, I was in North Minneapolis visiting my dear friend Amanda, an elderly woman I would visit each month or so. We had become friends across the generations. It was August 8, 1974. I would never remember that particular date except that a news flash came on television as we were visiting and chatting. We watched the coverage all afternoon, aghast, as the president of the United States resigned on national television. It was an incredible moment for us to share."

Within a few short months, all of their lives would be swept into the vortex of Bob Dylan's obsessive quest to produce a work of unimpeachable quality.

CHAPTER
FOUR

WHEN JOHN HAMMOND PHONED, you dropped everything and took the call. A fixture at Columbia Records for as long as anyone could remember, Hammond was an industry legend whose A&R skills had transformed the course of popular music for four decades. A soft-left civil rights egalitarian whose social and political attitudes had been forged during the Great Depression of the '30s, he had been the driving force behind the From Spirituals to Swing concerts held at Carnegie Hall over the Christmases of 1938 and 1939, at which a racially integrated (but largely white) audience was introduced to the wide range of black music percolating from the "race records" ghetto.

By any standards, these were extraordinary shows: Headlined by Count Basie's Orchestra, the 1938 lineup offered gospel (Sister Rosetta Tharpe and Mitchell's Christian Singers), Dixieland jazz (Sidney Bechet leading the New Orleans Feetwarmers), ragtime piano (James P. Johnson), country blues (Big Bill Broonzy), harmonica blues (Sonny Terry), big-band blues (Jimmy Rushing), and boogie-woogie piano

(Meade Lux Lewis, Albert Ammons, Pete Johnson), as well as the innovative pairing of Big Joe Turner with Pete Johnson, plus a segment by Basie's small Kansas City Five combo featuring Lester Young. A year later, a similar lineup was joined by Jubilee gospel stars, the Golden Gate Quartet, and the Benny Goodman Sextet—an awesome combo featuring Lionel Hampton, Charlie Christian, and Fletcher Henderson—the show being crowned by a lengthy jam session in which members of Goodman's and Basie's bands were joined by Lewis and Ammons for an extended series of solos.

Having thus earned the respect of the black music community, Hammond was able to parlay these connections into a groundbreaking series of signings of such seminal artists as Benny Goodman and Billie Holiday, coups that enabled Columbia to become the preeminent jazz outlet of the '40s and '50s. In later years, he was also the first major-label player to recognize the potential of Aretha Franklin—though so in thrall was Columbia at the time to the easy-listening hegemony established by A&R chief Mitch Miller that the label had no clear idea how best to present Aretha, and it was only when she jumped ship to Ahmet Ertegun's more sympathetic Atlantic Records that she went on to megastardom.

Hammond's greatest gamble, however, was his signing of Bob Dylan, a performer whose scruffy appearance, harsh nasal whine, and bluesy style were so contrary to the prevailing wholesome, clean-cut image of folk musicians established in the late '50s by The Kingston Trio. For a white Jewish kid, he sounded awfully "black" to some of Hammond's colleagues, and how were they going to sell that? So alien were Dylan's talents to the company that he was for a while referred to in the corridors of Columbia as "Hammond's Folly"—though only until his second album, *The Freewheelin' Bob Dylan*, jump-started the whole folk-protest boom and transformed the course of popular music.

By 1974, however, Hammond's better days were considered by many at the company to be behind him—few, for instance, had much faith in his latest signing, Bruce Springsteen, whose second album had recently performed little better than his debut, despite Columbia's attempts to market the wordy New Jersey rocker as "the new Dylan"—but he still wielded sufficient clout to bring Phil Ramone to the phone when he called him at A&R Studios in New York on September 13. Ramone was glad he took the call. "Dylan's in town," said Hammond, "and we need to capture something magical about him."

Phil Ramone is one of the music industry's top producer/engineers, who, since starting his career in 1963 with Lesley Gore's No. 1 hit, "It's My Party," has worked with an impressive roster of artists, including Frank Sinatra, Barbra Streisand, Billy Joel, Elton John, and Quincy Jones. He had been sound engineer on Dylan's 1974 tour and had spent the summer with producer Rob Fraboni, editing the concert tapes and assembling the performances that would become the *Before the Flood* live album. But it was Ramone's work the year before on Paul Simon's highly acclaimed solo album, *There Goes Rhymin' Simon*, that had marked him out as a producer with a particular sensitivity to the needs of singer-songwriters, and as a shrewd choice to work on Dylan's next sessions.

"John said that Bob was going to be in town and was insisting on using the old Columbia A studio on 54th Street, which then was called A&R Recording," says Ramone. "This was a period of A&R's life that was amazing: The Paul Simons and the Sinatras, all these people, had been recording at this studio. And Dylan had an incredible love for this room, which had been sold by Columbia. A group of us, including me, ended up buying the studio, and we made a few changes, but not too many. It was a big room, just like a church, with a huge, high ceiling.

"I think there was a feeling of Bob coming back to Columbia, and to his friendship with John. I had just made a song with Paul Simon, called 'Me and Julio Down by the Schoolyard,' and I think the thing that starts getting handed off from one artist to another is the fact that I was, let's say, singer-songwriter-oriented—I think my whole reputation came from that kind of thing. John Hammond and [Columbia producer] Don DeVito were boosting my new career." The session was lined up for the evening of September 16, three days later.

If Ramone was lined up at short notice, the musicians had even less time to prepare. On the morning of the 16th, guitarist and banjo player Eric Weissberg was up at A&R Studios working on an advertising jingle when he bumped into Phil Ramone in the hall.

Weissberg had become smitten with music—and especially the banjo—as a child at a Catskills summer camp, Camp Woodland, when folk music legend Pete Seeger came to play for the kids, and he had subsequently studied violin at New York's High School of Music and Art before becoming a bass major at the Juilliard School of Music. His plans to become a symphonic bassist were derailed when he joined the folk group The Tarriers in 1959, touring with them for six years before joining Judy Collins's band for the next year or two. Weissberg's and Dylan's paths had crossed occasionally during the '60s folk music boom—at the same time that Dylan was dating Suze Rotolo, his cover costar on the front sleeve of *The Freewheelin' Bob Dylan*, Weissberg was dating her sibling, Carla, the "parasite sister" so viciously denigrated in Dylan's "Ballad in Plain D"—though they never really hung out together much.

After his stint with Judy Collins, Weissberg decided to become a session musician, upending a couple of lean years building up a reputation as a reliable and versatile player. "I was very lucky to come along when I did," Weissberg believes, "because I was just about the only guy who could play all the folk instruments—mandolin, fiddle, Dobro, etc.—*and* read music and follow a chart." By 1974, he was sufficiently well established on the studio scene to be making a six-figure income from it.

When he met Phil Ramone at A&R Studios, Weissberg was on a hot streak following the success of the 1973 movie *Deliverance,* for which he had written and recorded a banjo instrumental, "Dueling Banjos," which had become a tremendous worldwide hit. The success of the movie had helped the single, and vice versa, so Eric had formed a group made up of drummer Richard Crooks, guitarist Charlie Brown III, and bass player Tony Brown to tour the country in support of the recording. "We had a lot of fun going out on weekends and honking, and then zipping back into the studios during the week," he recalls. "Another side effect of 'Dueling Banjos' was that there were a lot of copycat jingles using 'Dueling Banjos'–type music because of it, and I probably got to play almost all of them. And right then, every session I went to, I was greeted by all the session guys playing it at me in fun when I walked in! It was more than nice."

Ramone buttonholed Weissberg in the hall.

"Eric, do you have a band?" he asked.

"Yes, you know the guys—Charlie and Crooks, Tom Mc-Faul, Tony Brown," answered Weissberg. "Why?"

"Well, Bob is recording tonight," said Ramone, "but we don't have a band."

Weissberg wasn't about to pass up an opportunity like that and told Ramone he would call the guys and see if they could make it on such short notice.

Eric's first call went to Charlie Brown, a seasoned session guitarist whose pedigree included records by Solomon Burke, James Brown, Van Morrison, Barbra Streisand, Engelbert Humperdinck, and Johnny Cash. "The word got to us through Eric that we'd got this gig," he recalls. "I don't even remember whether we knew it was with Dylan, because dates just happened, y'know? Mainly jingles for commercials—sometimes at the rate of four a day. I did a lot for companies like Quaker Oats and Burger King—I wrote a couple, too: I wrote the first Black & Decker Workmate spot, for that little fold-up table, and some Burger King things. The Dylan session, I remember, was at 799 Seventh

Avenue, the old Columbia Studios, which were huge, especially the main studio. Phil Ramone and Don Frey now operated it as A&R Studios—Don is an old friend of my sister's, and he was handling the business, while Phil was still doing engineering."

Richard Crooks and Tony Brown were likewise available, as was keyboardist Tom McFaul, who had become friends with Weissberg through playing sessions together. Most of McFaul's work came from the advertising business—indeed, so successful was he at writing, arranging, playing, and producing music for television commercials that he had his own production company and recording studio—but he was prepared to make an exception in Dylan's case.

The others were just as eager. Though he was an experienced player who had backed many folk and blues musicians—he played on Dr. John's *Gumbo,* for instance, and a lot of Loudon Wainwright III's songs, including the hit single "Dead Skunk," and subsequently became part of Leonard Cohen's touring band—drummer Richard Crooks was equally excited about the prospect of working with a living legend.

"Eric called me up and said, 'Hey, we're gonna go and record with Dylan,'" he recalls. "I was pretty enthused and excited about it all. Between you and me, I've always respected him as a poet and storyteller, though I was never really a big Dylan fan. But hey, we were in the recording business in New York, and I thought this would be fun to do. It was in the midst of recording mayhem, one in a long line of sessions we were doing. You'd work eight or ten com mercial jobs during the day—the recording scene in New York in the '70s was just a madhouse: If you're on the lists of the writers or arrangers or producers, whoever, you were working constantly, as much as you'd think your body could stand. So when I asked Eric what the session was for, and he told me it was for Dylan, that was a great buzz. But we were only there for three days and then we were gone, off working on something else."

About half an hour before the session was due to start, the musicians arrived at A&R Studios to prepare. Weissberg unpacked and tuned his prize guitar, a 1939 Martin Herringbone D-28 he had purchased on the Lower East Side at Harry Newcorn's music store.

"Eric called me and said we were doing a session with Dylan," recalls bassist Tony Brown. "I was totally excited. I was a huge fan." Adds Weissberg, "There was a certain excitement happening in the studio while Phil and we were setting up."

McFaul agrees. "It was certainly a unique experience for all of us," he says. "I was nervous. I didn't know what to expect, and I became more nervous as things progressed."

Charlie Brown tuned his powerful Fender Telecaster guitar for the sessions, feeling "nervous, because Dylan had been one of my big heroes forever. Eric actually knew him— not that well, but Eric knows *everybody*. I was excited about playing with Dylan."

Having worked with Dylan on the Before the Flood tour, Ramone had a shrewd idea of what was required to capture the mercurial artist at his best.

"I happen to have used the technique at the time, which is nothing unusual, but comes out great in 5.1, of using two guitar mikes," he explains, "for reasons of sound and to give him freedom of movement, because he's not prone to stand in one place without moving around, y'know? One was a Sony C37, a tube mike; the other was a Neumann KM56. I think I tried something different on the vocals, because I went to a dynamic mike, a Sennheiser 421, rather than a condenser mike, mainly because I felt I could get around his movement better.

"We had pretty good isolation," Ramone continues. "You hear his voice in his guitar mike, as you would anyone's, but leakage is important, and the leakage in the guitar mike was quite good. It expands the voice, and it can either expand it negatively, or it can expand it in a whole other direction, because of the interaction of the three mikes. Normally people stay away from that, but I was never a traditionalist in the way things were recorded. I felt the most important thing was to capture the guy's motif in the room, and not stiffly, as in a typical studio where you can't move much. I'm known for being a bit crazy in putting mikes into Mick Jagger's and Frank Sinatra's hands, because if you do move, the most important thing is to try and be comfortable in the studio. And Bob is not much of a conversant guy—you use what you believe is the best; there's no trial and error. I didn't want to have a situation with the mike, and looking back and trying to figure why I did this, it was possibly because condenser mikes have a valve in them, which could sweat or crackle suddenly; but for whatever reason, I didn't use anything but a dynamic mike on his vocals.

"It helped with the isolation, too: I'd been through this for years before, with Peter, Paul & Mary, and with Paul Simon: How do you keep the vocal out of the guitar mike, or vice versa? And I'd found that a dynamic mike with a reasonably good rejection in the back helps. That's probably one of the reasons. The Sennheiser 421 was a popular stage mike back then: We used that a lot with The Band. It's a forgotten mike in many ways—it looks like a long bullet, almost like a little crate, a little coffin. They were hugely popular in rock 'n' roll, often used to get good isolation on a drumkit, though to me they were too big for that and could easily be hit with a drumstick. But the damage on that mike wasn't the same cost of an expensive Neumann. But it had an interesting top end, a warmth, if you kept reasonably close to it."

Ramone strove to capture the sound as cleanly and simply as possible, with only the slightest touch of reverb added.

"The reverb is Seventh Avenue, as it was called," he explains. "The room was big, but downstairs we had some incredibly good chambers. There's just a touch of the room, and I was coming out of my overecho days—or maybe I was just coming back to them, I don't know!—but the room had life, and just a small amount of reverb added to it gave it extra life. In the new 5.1 surround mix, the effect of how the room continues on after the note is very subtle—you can hear that in the rear speakers."

The only information Ramone had obtained prior to the session had come in the phone call from John Hammond. "When I got that call, he said, 'Maybe you need a bass player, but I don't think you'll need drums—we'll just have the bass player figure out the parts,'" remembers Ramone. "Well, Bob doesn't rehearse; Bob just starts creating! These songs start pouring out of him, and the bass player's looking at me like, 'What's wrong with you? Excuse me, but can I write these charts down?' I said, 'He won't do it the same way twice, he might throw a 2/4 bar in there or suddenly go to the next part of the verse without the normal turnaround song form.' Most songs have some kind of shape, but his shapes were so unpredictable and wonderful that the musicians had to learn a lot on the date."

This is something of an understatement. Ever the gentleman, Weissberg today reflects, "The session was a bit bizarre for us."

"This is how it got started. Bob came into A&R studio A1 and immediately called us to the center of the room, where he began playing and singing the first tune. We scrambled for paper and pencils to try and scribble down the changes and the road map, etc. I don't know which song it was, but it had a lot of verses, and we each got our own chart scratched out. Then I think we ran it down once, maybe twice, and Bob asked Phil if he was ready to record.

"Phil grumbled a bit and then said, 'OK, go ahead,' and we did our first take. Bob asked for a playback. This was a fairly large studio, big enough for a symphony orchestra, and there were playback speakers the size of refrigerators.

Ample playback sound. During the playback, Bob called us to gather around him again and started to run down the next song. Yikes!"

Charlie Brown felt somewhat helpless, and he was not alone. "He didn't use any charts," says the guitarist. "I finally wound up getting a yellow legal pad and scribbling down a couple of things, which were gone, instantly, right out the window. It wasn't worth bothering to write them down, he changed things so much.

"It's not that he's wrong; it's just that it's a whole other way of thinking from what we were used to. He would run something down once, and maybe halfway again, and that was it: Take it! Because he wanted the immediacy of the moment—he didn't care whether there were mistakes in there or not; that's just the way it happened. We, on the other hand, were used to getting it right. We called mistakes 'clams'— 'I'm sorry man, I just made a clam on bar 34, should we retake, or else I'll overdub it later, what do you think?' Even when Deliverance got together for a rehearsal, we'd beat ourselves up pretty good, y'know, to make sure we got it right. And then we play with him, and he's like a bad boxer, he's throwing punches all over the place, and we're just trying to get out of the way! Eric and I would listen back and hear the mistakes and want to fix them, but we weren't allowed to."

Weissberg was concerned for his reputation. "Since mistakes had been made by each of us, we pleaded for another take, appealing to Bob in a nice 'We're on this record too, give us another chance to do it right' manner," he says. "We did another take and then moved on reasonably well and nicely, through, I think, another four or five songs. I remember having a pretty good time and feeling good about the whole thing the more it went on."

The priorities for the session quickly became apparent. "My job was to make sure Bob was comfortable at the microphone, make sure his earphones were working, and just start recording," says Phil Ramone, outlining the approach that would later be emulated by his admiring disciple, sound engineer Paul Martinson, at Sound 80 Studio in Minneapolis. "I've been a part of some momentous occasions where you prepare your studio and yourself and then wait and watch; and sometimes, what I thought was the rundown turned out to be the performance. So if a basement tape was made, or something like that, we could punch in and fix any mistakes. I sat the bass player where he could see Dylan's hands, but if Dylan moved his hands to another chord suddenly, the bass part would be wrong at that point, so we would punch it in later. But we only punched in things like a bass part or an organ note that went sour. Not on him. Definitely not on him! And I never stopped a take. That's the kind of thing you don't do. There's a certain teaching that comes down from the Clint Eastwoods and the Frank Sinatras: They're *prepared*. Bob has probably sat for days thinking about what he's doing, and the last thing he needs to do is worry about the technology in the room. Because the momentum is what counts in a song, the momentum and the revelation of how you feel as you're singing it."

"You can't discard when you're working with Bob Dylan—or anybody, really," he adds. "But when you're in that mode you're listening very carefully, for things as simple as, is that guitar OK, is it in tune, if not, should I stop, no, go forward. You can hear noises on this record that you typically would have said, Let's do another take: His pick gets going on one or two songs, for example. I was able to reduce some of it, but that's almost part of the character, like the rattling mike-stand: The next take, I would put a sandbag on the foot of the stand, but the take is there; there's no 'C'mon, Bob, we need another one' just because the engineer wasn't paying attention."

In other words, everything possible was done to make the session easy for Dylan, which didn't necessarily make it easier for the musicians. For one thing, he wouldn't always stick to a song, switching to another if he felt it wasn't working quite right or needed something else.

"He would almost make a medley of them," recalls Ramone. "He'd go into the second song sometimes, and maybe a third, then come back to the first."

It was a chastening experience for Charlie Brown in particular. "I thought, what a treat this was going to be, man," he recalls. "And as it turned out, it was and it wasn't. In the middle of something, he would just turn around and say, 'Stop! Okay, I'm going to do *this* now,' and just turn right back around and go into it again. The only way you could tell what he was doing was to watch his hands, and the guitar player, me or Eric, would have to say, 'It's in E' or whatever, and bang, hit it! And sometimes it was in E, and sometimes it wasn't. He'd sort of scuffle around for a couple of bars, and somebody would hold up a hand that looked like an E, or an A, or whatever. But that was it—he was real quick; he just wanted to go in and do it.

"We never did more than two takes of any song. And every time we'd go into the booth to listen back to it, I don't think he ever listened back to anything the whole way through: Either he'd say, 'I don't like that' or 'There's something wrong with it'—I think he was generally referring to his own performance, because he would say, 'Erase that,' meaning, 'Go back and record over the top of it,' the reason being, I imagine, that there were so many bootleg recordings of Dylan around that he just didn't want that to happen anymore, so he would just erase everything."

"He'd say things like 'It's too refined' or 'I can't come off that shiny,'" adds Richard Crooks. "He'd prefer to be a little more roguish or devil-may-care, which is why he does takes differently. He'll do one take of one song, then just move on to another song, and maybe an hour or two later he'll come back and do that first song again, just so you don't lock in on it too much. He likes that loose, unpredictable feel, rather than the 'We've practiced this song for a week, look how well we do it' approach. He just doesn't seem to want to come off sounding so musically brilliant—and he really is! There's so much more underlying this frivolous, sort of devil-may-care, grasping-for-chords stuff."

Despite all the difficulties they had to face in accompanying him, all the players found Dylan pleasant and easy to get along with. "His mood ranged from very personal to slightly imperious," says Tom McFaul. "For example, he asked us if we wanted to go on the road with him—he said he wanted

to play only prisons. We all said yes, of course! When he became impatient, he used the courtly 'we,' rather than 'I,' as
in 'We don't want the *piano,* we want the *organ,*' or 'We
don't like that take, erase it.'

"There was virtually no rehearsal. Dylan would play part
of a song; then he'd say, 'It's got a bridge, like any other
bridge, you'll get it'; then we would record."

"It was a very relaxed ambience," recalls Crooks. "The
only uptightness was caused by the fact that everybody felt
this 'I'm here with Bob Dylan!' vibe. But as far as the work
process went, it was totally relaxed: We'd go in, play a song,
sit around and bullshit for half an hour, play another song,
listen back. . . ."

The lack of feedback about their performances, however,
and their inability to adjust the recording methods to allevi-
ate the problems they were facing became a source of annoyance to Charlie Brown in particular.

"There was a little bit of funny stuff going on," he says, "in
that Phil Ramone—who was, and is, a wonderful engineer—
was treating Dylan like he was Elvis Presley. And I suppose,
y'know, rightfully so, maybe; but what I mean is that things
would not be going quite right—and Deliverance were all studio players and used to getting it exactly right. We would go in
and say something occasionally—I said something a couple of
times, and so did everybody else, asking him, 'Can you get
Bob to do this?'—whatever it was—and Ramone never
opened his mouth, never responded. It drove me crazy."

Ramone, of course, had an entirely different set of priorities from the musicians. All musicians, whether playing in

bands or on sessions, suffer from a kind of aural myopia that prevents them, when first listening back to a recording, from hearing anything except their own contribution. Ask the guitarist what he thought of the drum part, or vice versa, and he'll just look puzzled: You mean there were drums on this, too? Hence the need for a producer, for an objective ear that can perceive the whole sound picture without being distracted by the detail. In this instance, Ramone was particularly mindful of the need to preserve Dylan's creative mood and was determined not to fracture it with pointless, irritating interruptions.

"I sort of understood that, from the people I'd worked with before—I'd worked as an engineer with Sinatra, and so on—you really get to know that their privacy is probably the most important thing you get to deal with," he explains. "When you're in the role of engineer/producer, it's because you have an affinity to their music, and you take on a different role accordingly, either very vocal or, in Bob's case, very quiet. I really believe that critical to anybody's relationship is how you manage to stay out of the way as the music is coming in—it's not fun to be chatty and silly all over the place.

"Bob's a serious guy. This was a serious night. This was a very quiet, deliberate letting out of the inside of him. Emotionally he was in a state of revealing his life, and most writers don't want to tell you they're writing their autobiography, but it's there in the atmosphere, as you hear the songs unfolding."

Charlie Brown was unimpressed with Ramone's softly-softly approach. "He never said a damn word the whole time we were in there," he says. "He just pushed a few faders around and sat back with his arms behind his head. I know Phil is a good engineer and producer, but I gotta tell ya, the people that he has produced and recorded are some of the best artists on the planet, so he didn't have to do a whole lot of producing, just push a few faders and shut the hell up!"

In his defense, Ramone could cite the influence of his mentor John Hammond, whose relationship with Dylan he had been able to observe over a period of time and learn from.

"My hero, from a producer's point of view, was John Hammond," he affirms. "Watching that relationship, the trust between those two guys, allowed me into something. Of course, it's an historic album, but beyond that, it taught me how you make your career grow because of people like Dylan—you learn things like, how do you shut your mouth? When do you speak? *Why* do you speak? Make sure that when you do open your mouth, you have something to say other than 'Nice weather,' y'know?"

For all his discontent, Brown managed to cope. "It was a fairly relaxed process, once we figured out what Bob was doing," he says. "We had never worked with him before— Eric had, but I had no idea what I was going to run into. I thought Bob would be a bit of a stickler for getting a certain sound, but the way he got that certain sound was by not being a stickler. So we just let her rip, watching his hands so we could know we were in the right place."

"I didn't realize the kind of way that Dylan went at stuff," adds Richard Crooks. "He never played the same thing the same way twice, which left me disoriented and discombobulated. On the other hand, it was great, because you had to be flexible, musically speaking." Just as flexible, it transpired, as Dylan himself, who demonstrated a command of music theory and technique that impressed even these seasoned session players.

"I never thought of Dylan as much of a musician," Crooks admits, "but one thing that came up in that session was that this guy was unbelievable: As well as having a phenomenal memory for lyrics, he had a good grasp of musical technique. He would say, 'Ah, I don't like it in that key,' and change to another, but he never capo'd anything on the guitar. He would bar-chord the changes; we probably went through six or seven different keys on just one song, and he never capo'd anything, he had all the transpositions right there, bang, bang, bang, bang! Holy mackerel!

"I didn't know he had that power, because if you listen to some of the stuff he does, it's very simple in terms of the playing and chord structures. But he could do anything he wanted, at a moment's notice—most guys would be sitting around figuring it out for a while, but he just did it straight off. His musicality was just astounding; as simple as it seems, there was a whole lot more happening than meets the eye. One night he was in his cups, so bombed you'd think he wouldn't be able to play, but he was still going through the changes smoothly."

"That's true," affirms Charlie Brown. "Some of them had quite a few changes, too, and he would just go to them like you'd expect any good studio player to, but you don't think of Bob Dylan as being any kind of a monster player. He's actually a lot better than people know. But if he's not playing with a drummer, if he's just singing and playing guitar, his tempos do tend to follow his voice—but then, so do mine."

Notwithstanding the musicians' respect for Dylan's abilities, however, the circumstances of the session setup posed tough problems for them.

"Studio A1 was a big room—you could put a sixty-piece orchestra in there, no problem—and it also sounded fantastic in there," remembers Charlie Brown. "They had a live set-up for Bob, with a guitar microphone and a vocal microphone live there in the room, and all the other guitar players and Tom McFaul, the organist, we were all right there behind him in the room, and they took Richard Crooks and put him in a drum booth. Now, in order to hear Richard, you've got to wear your headphones, and Bob didn't want to wear headphones. So how do you do that? I guess you have to put Bob's guitar way up in the phones and simply follow him, which was not that easy, because he tends to shift tempos with his lyrics. We complained a little about that, and I don't remember what really happened, but I seem to recall Richard eventually just kicking the damn door open, or something like that, so we could hear him in the room.

"I had to wear headphones, because I was twenty feet away from Bob, and half the time I couldn't see his hands. If I could see his hands, then I could kind of go where he was going—but Tom McFaul had his back to him, and he couldn't see a thing. And even if he did see his hands, he wouldn't be able to tell what was going on."

Being used to the smoothly rigorous procedures employed in recording advertising jingles, Tom McFaul was the most inconvenienced by the extempore methods used at the Dylan sessions.

"I have never been involved in such a bizarre recording set-up before or since, even with the most eccentric artists," he claims. "We all knew Phil Ramone, of course, and had worked with him before, but he had set up the cue so that we could not hear ourselves or one another at all. Only Dylan was in the cue, playing and singing at the same time. This, of course, seemed absurd. I think we all felt that we should have said something about the way things were going down. I think we all felt we were extremely limited in what we could contribute because of the weird recording set-up.

"Under normal circumstances, this cue situation would not be tolerated by the players. But no one said anything. At one point I heard the assistant engineer whisper to Phil that the snare drum mike was not working. Phil just waved him off. I realized later that Ramone was only interested in getting Dylan on tape. It didn't matter what any of us played. That could be dealt with later."

Charlie Brown was equally disillusioned. "I agree with Tom on that," he says, "and I guess I thought it was going to be much more than that, that we were going to be a band, playing behind Bob Dylan. And it wasn't like that at all. In fact, I wonder why anybody bothered calling for a band at all. Seriously! Bob could just have stood there and done it on his own, and then a band could have been overdubbed behind him."

But Ramone was fully aware of what he needed to do and how to get the job done. "Formally trained people get a little thrown by it," he admits, but he believes that's not necessarily a bad thing in itself. "It makes everybody come to life: You're on your toes, you're watching, you're listening, you're hearing everything. A lot of artists work from a free-form attitude, and the discipline is to know where the bass line might be; once the parts get created, then later that day, or the day after, you start to add and subtract them.

"But I think what's incredibly unusual about Bob is the fact that it flows in a most natural way. Now, Paul Simon also flows, but Paul has found a discipline: When he likes something, then we notate it, and that becomes the pattern (although I've seen Paul also drop bars where he feels the emotion of the song needs to get to someplace quicker). Bob is less likely to do that. Though I must preface that with the fact that at the time, *Blood on the Tracks* was an outpouring of the man's life, in a very troubled time for him, and this was almost cathartic for him in the studio. It was incredible. Nobody stopped, nobody said anything, nobody talked very much: It certainly wasn't a social gathering, it was more of a soul being revealed directly to tape."

Crooks concurs. "I knew Phil from a long time back," he recalls. "Phil's a great guy, a very talented man. I knew him when he was just an engineer, before he really got any kind of name, before he had that success with Billy Joel. I was with Rhinoceros, an old rock group that he was thinking about producing, so we went in the studio for two or three days with Phil. He just had a way of knowing what the essence of a certain situation was, how many takes to do, knowing exactly what he needed to make the record sound good. So many producers will approach things in a very exacting manner—'I want this note exactly here, and this note exactly there,' like Steely Dan kind of stuff, everything plotted out perfectly; and while it works for Steely Dan, for others it often comes out sounding contrived, overproduced. Phil just had this way of knowing when he'd got enough takes for his final mix, when it felt good, and a little fluff here and there didn't make that much difference.

"It was only difficult in that you never knew what Dylan was going to do next. We'd record a song one way; then he'd say, 'Let's just do another take,' and you'd think you knew where everything was, and all of a sudden the second take would be a little bit different from the one we'd just done before. You couldn't rely on there being a predictable set of chord changes all the time; you had to be free-flowing enough to go with the flow: not think it out too much but use your ears and trust your instincts and abilities. Which is why he surrounded himself with great musicians—Weissberg was a phenomenal player, and Charlie Brown and Tony Brown were great musicians too. Bob would just say, 'Let's go,' 1–2–3–4, and everybody would start playing, and it wouldn't necessarily be the same."

"I think, in the end, Ramone understood this and wisely kept recording, regardless of what the band was doing," concedes Tom McFaul. "We would record before we had run

down a song even once. There was no music, of course. The
guitar players could kind of look at Dylan's hands and see
where he was going. I don't play the guitar, so that was no
help to me. I don't have perfect pitch either, so I would go up
to the piano to find out what key he was in. Dylan would
stop me: 'We don't want the piano, we want the organ.' 'I
know,' I would say, 'I'm just trying to figure out what key we
are . . .' 'We don't want the *piano,* we want the *organ.*' Yes,
sir! I would go back to the B-3, which was way on the other
side of the studio, and which I could not hear, and hope like
hell we were in A major. None of us could hear a thing we
were playing, or anything anyone else was playing. I could
see the drummer, in the booth, but it was like a mime act."

Eric Weissberg doesn't recall exactly what was recorded
on that first night. "I don't remember which songs we did,"
he says, "except I guess one was the title song [presumably
he means 'Idiot Wind,' which contains the phrase 'blood on
your saddle']. As with a lot of Bob's songs, you don't get the
full meaning right away, and we were concentrating on our
parts rather intensely, to say the least. I did enjoy all the
songs in any case, even if I had little idea what they were
about! Phil was always relaxed, helpful, and keeping things
light, while Bob was intense and seemed a bit ill at ease in
the studio, as though he wanted to get it over with. Maybe
he was always like that in the studio, I don't know. It didn't
matter to us."

When the session finished, the musicians drifted off into
the night, both elevated and enervated by the experience of
backing Dylan. It had been a long and trying evening, and

some of them adjourned to a nearby hostelry for a pick-me-up. "Richard and I had been roommates many years on the road, and I can probably guess we hit the nearest bar," says Charlie Brown. "And there was one right across the street." In the bar, they bitched good-naturedly about the session, as musicians are wont to do after being put through the mill.

"We did have a chuckle about it afterward," says Richard Crooks. "Charlie was the kind of guy who really liked to formulate everything, to get everything together, and he was constantly ranting and raving about it: 'The guy never played the same thing twice, goddammit! I don't care who the hell he is, he never played the same chords!' Obviously, as a drummer I don't have to worry about the chords, it's much easier for me—though he would drop a beat here and there; but when you're playing chords, it's a little difficult if you're clashing with the guy—it's sort of like mind reading.

"The *power* of this guy was fascinating," he adds. "The stuff that he would do! Everybody would say, 'Oh, that's great, Bob,' even when it sucked. Everybody was yessin' him. Though I gained a lot of respect for the guy; in another way I kinda went away thinking, 'Wow—this is the great Bob Dylan? What a schmuck!' The power of this guy, and how much he could get away with, how everybody was just walking on eggshells around him all the time, not to mess with Bob. He's a strong individual. Nobody would go up to him and say, 'Bob, that sounded like shit!'"

Crooks does, however, balance his judgment of Dylan's working methods with this recollection, a prime example of the kind of sarcastic wit the singer had wielded so cuttingly in his younger days. "There was one phrase I overheard that really stuck with me," he recalls. "Someone was giving him advice, telling him, 'Bob, if you did this and that it might be better,' and he said, 'Y'know, if I'd listened to everybody who told me how to do stuff, I might *be* somewhere by now.' I thought, 'Oh my God, you got *that* right, brother!' It was terrific!"

Charlie Brown, meanwhile, was less than enamored of Phil Ramone's work behind the console.

"I hate to say this, but I ain't too fond of Phil," he says. "I think he took a lot of credit for stuff that I don't think he did. Producing all these people and having his name on it as producer is bullshit, because he didn't *do* anything, y'know? My idea of a producer is someone like Bert Berns, who was about as active as you could get—he would guide things, he would hire the people, he would make the whole thing happen, and he wouldn't think twice about stopping a take and saying, 'Let's do that again, but like this'—he was like a producer/arranger/engineer, and that's what I like to see in somebody who's calling themselves a producer."

In Tom McFaul's view, "Each take was a performance. Dylan played and sang as if it were a live gig, rather than a recording session." True to "live gig" form, Dylan recorded an amazing thirty takes on the first New York session, including the basic track for "Meet Me in the Morning" that would appear on the final release of *Blood on the Tracks* four months later, enhanced by Buddy Cage's steel guitar overdubs. Two further songs from this session also saw the light of day two decades later on *The Bootleg Series, Vol-*

umes 1–3, namely, the first version of "Tangled Up in Blue," which concluded the evening's work, and "Call Letter Blues," an early version of "Meet Me in the Morning."

"We made a pretty good collection of the songs that night," reckons Phil Ramone. "I always ran a mix as we were recording, because many times when you go back and try to change the equation, it changes everything. I still tell people, what I made here is the reason that I like the take and bought the take—I felt that way then, because when you're working with a Dylan, he's not waiting around to overdub.

"I truly didn't think there was going to be that much to alter—I had made a few quick fixes that night, or toward the end of the week; John Hammond had said to me, 'What do you think of this, because we're missing a few words here, or his guitar gets strident here,' or something—that kind of fix, not what I'd call a remix fix. I was very careful, because I knew the room so well—it was like my baby, that room, I knew its idiosyncrasies—and anyway, you were supposed to mix well on the date, you weren't supposed to have to remix; it wasn't a luxury that people wanted you to have. I felt that if you were confident, and he was happy, and it sounded right, that was it: You just put together whatever takes they wanted, and off you go. And whatever complications and ideas and options that you have in today's digital studios, you still have to play it as a mix: Someone, somewhere has to hear this as a composite of what the artist had in mind or what you're doing as a producer. That's also how we worked with The Band on the road: It's the essence of a concert—Was the better night Monday or Thursday?—rather than 'Let's recut it.'"

The sessions would continue for another few nights, but with only bassist Tony Brown retained from the Deliverance band for the subsequent sessions. Although some published versions of a purported studio cue sheet also listed Barry Kornfeld on guitar, he was not in attendance and did not play on *Blood on the Tracks* with Eric Weissberg's group.

"I know we were there for one real long session, and then Tony did a bunch, two or three days after that," says Charlie Brown. "It's all kind of a big jumble." "What was even stranger and more exciting was after the first session (September 16)," says Tony Brown. "I got a call from someone in Dylan's office who said 'come on back.' I asked, was Eric going to be there, and the guys? The person said, 'No, just you.' That was a shock. I had no idea why that was. I was more nervous then."

When the sessions continued late on September 17, Dylan cut his "performance" in half, condensing it to sixteen takes. This time, two songs made it to the Columbia release of *Blood on the Tracks*, namely "Shelter from the Storm" and "You're Gonna Make Me Lonesome When You Go." An early version of "You're a Big Girl Now" was included on the original Columbia test pressing but was later replaced by one recorded in Minneapolis three months later.

At the full band sessions, according to Charlie, "Nobody was loaded, but there was a little bit of moonshine sitting over on the corner shelf, and I was certainly imbibing, as was everybody. So we're all out there, and we're all feeling kinda happy now; we don't care *what* he does! Bob gets into this tune, I don't remember which it was, and we're all just wailin', and Bob never forgot a lyric; he was perfect every time—and you know what Bob's lyrics are like, they're *books*—but not once did he miss; but he leaned in a little too far once and caught his guitar on the guitar mike and broke the third string.

"Now, third string is about the size of a telephone pole on one of those acoustics; you just don't do that! He took one look at it and said something like 'Damn! I don't feel like changing that.' and I said, 'Okay,' and went over and changed it for him—I don't know he was even aware I changed it; he just picked it up and started playing again. The whole thing was funny, and fun at the same time; I didn't find him to be a bad guy, or hard to get along with at all: He was easy to talk to when we took a break for a minute. He asked us if we wanted to go out and play some prisons with him, and we said, 'Sure, let's go!' but maybe the idea came back to him later and he took somebody else. We would have gone in a minute."

Charlie's attitude toward Dylan's working methods has softened with time, too. "It was so . . . I almost said 'unprofessional,' but it wasn't unprofessional; it was just another way of doing it," he now maintains. "Like Jackson Pollock, as opposed to, say, one of the impressionists who would take an inordinate amount of time getting it right, y'know? That's kinda how it felt to me. I didn't get the message until about three-quarters of the way through the first day, and then I thought, 'Oh, I know what he's doing: He just wants to hear whatever comes out.'"

During his one-on-one session on Septmeber 17, Tony Brown recalls Dylan's single-minded approach to the material. "He couldn't have been more remote. I can't remember any words that were spoken. He was concentrating entirely on the songs, nothing else."

Following Tony Brown's first lone session with Dylan on September 17, he was called back for another session two days later with Paul Griffin. The September 19 session proved extremely productive, the players demonstrating a chemistry not unlike what would develop between Dylan and drummer Bill Berg in Minneapolis three months later. Two of these takes appear on the final Columbia version of *Blood on the Tracks*, namely "Buckets of Rain" and "Simple Twist of Fate." Another track, "Up to Me"—effectively the same tune as "Shelter from the Storm," with a different lyric—appears on the *Biograph* box set.

"In those three or four nights," explains Ramone, "you have a way of saying, 'It would be great to do another take of "Idiot Wind,"' not because you're trying to be a perfectionist, but more because of the way it formed itself when the bass player played the right notes—because there's no information on paper, the bass player kept his eyes peeled on Dylan's hands all the time. And sometimes, Bob might go straight into a second verse with no amount of bars that were typical of how music was written, which gives you this incredible, shocking change. That's an interaction you can feel on the record, especially when there's an additional guitar or banjo or something—it's subtle, I put them in the back where they should be."

As Tony Brown worked with Dylan, recording nearly half the album in a single sitting, he thought to himself, "I am the first person to hear these songs, and they're great."

Tony Brown says, "What kept occurring to me during the sessions was, he's back; this material is really great. I tried not to stare at him, but because of the brilliance that was coming out of him, it was hard to avoid. I remember being struck by the songs. It was obvious to me what they were about, how deeply personal they were. I had a whole day with him, and the next day Paul Griffin was there."

During his sessions, Tony Brown "channeled" the bass playing from Dylan's *John Wesley Harding* album, which was, in his estimation, the last great album Dylan had made before *Blood on the Tracks*. "I made a conscious decision to emulate that style, and if you listen to 'You're Gonna Make Me Lonesome When You Go' and 'You're a Big Girl Now,' you'll hear it. I used a lot of eighth notes, just like Charlie McCoy played on *John Wesley Harding*. I really thought that what Paul Griffin and I did (September 19) was far superior to what was used on the final version of the album. Nothing can touch our version of 'Idiot Wind.' And I remember getting out of the sessions and telling people how great these new songs were."

The studio at 799 Seventh Avenue has since been demolished, taking with it the spiritual imprints of some of the last century's most notable recordings, a vast repository of pop, jazz, and folk history.

"I was by there recently and said, 'My God, didn't 799 used to be there?'" says Charlie Brown. "Like, a whole half a block was gone. A&R Studios were large and electronically state-of-the-art, but the rooms had some soul to them—you knew that thousands of wonderful people had played in there. They used to do a lot of jazz dates there when Columbia had hold of it, and there were pictures all over the wall of all the people who had played there; so every time I walked in the place I always felt really good about it."

Though he doubts it will happen, Phil Ramone would like to see the New York recordings, as mixed by him, given an official release by Columbia, possibly as part of the ongoing *Bootleg Series* of historic unreleased Dylan material.

"From an audience perspective, if Columbia puts this record out as it originally was," says Ramone, "even though it's got no extra goodies on it, it's that night, and I think if you're interested in Bob Dylan, that's going to be a landmark, in a sense that it's the original, as is. But throughout the years, there are certain outtakes of artists that I think should never have been released. And when possible, even though we weren't supposed to, I would erase them to prevent that. We used to joke about it—but then, if you pass away, they're going to put out everything they can find, including bad demos.

"Lyrically, it was an evening of unbelievable outpouring on a personal level—which doesn't mean you know it's going to sell or find a popularity level. Did I ever think it would become historic? No. I just thought it was a phase in a man's career: It's like running into a painting Picasso did in 1940, as opposed to one he did in 1950—the essence is what you feel, and when you're in the room engineering it and being part of the production, you definitely come up with feelings that are, you know . . ."

He pauses, momentarily lost for words, before finding the words that won't trample on Dylan's privacy: "They were tremendously sensitive areas."

CHAPTER
FIVE

THE FIRST TIME BUDDY CAGE HEARD Bob Dylan's "Like a Rolling Stone," he almost crashed his dad's car. At the time, Buddy was just starting out on a career in music, his head full of teenage dreams, and had secured an audition for a job backing a country singer from Buffalo called Jack Kingston, who had a lucrative contract playing shows for airmen and ground crews at Strategic Air Command bases.

"So I'm driving to this audition in my dad's '59 Oldsmobile, listening to the AM radio, and I'm hearing this brand-new song, 'Like a Rolling Stone,'" he recalls. "I had heard Dylan before, doing these talking-blues things and stuff, that I thought were very interesting and very strange; I really got a kick out of 'em, although I wasn't that much of a folk freak then. But when I listened to 'Like a Rolling Stone,' I was, like, Jesus Christ! I was physically ill! I had to pull the car over to the curb, park it, and just listen to this thing, stunned. It was like Bob had just opened this huge door to the galaxy and said, 'There you go.'"

Buddy got the gig with Jack Kingston, but he always kept one eye, and one ear, on that huge door from then on, ever alert for the wider opportunities at large in the musical galaxy. Which, being a pedal steel guitarist, weren't exactly that plentiful at the time.

"The instrument that I play is pigeonholed by people who see it pretty much as a country-and-western instrument—the odd train whistle here and there and chimes and shit," he says, with the exasperation of one who's suffered years of corny requests. "Well, I don't do chimes, and I don't do train whistles! I'm pretty much just a punk-ass street kid, and I don't put up with that crap—I'd rather be tossing coins in a hat! So I've been pretty much swimming upstream my whole life with that guitar, playing stuff that was outside and unconventional."

Luckily for Buddy, the outside and unconventional became prized musical commodities in the late 1960s, and once Dylan's *Nashville Skyline* had busted open the door for country rock, the early 1960s offered much more interesting opportunities for daring pedal steel players like himself, Al Perkins of The Flying Burrito Brothers, and Orville "Red" Rhodes of ex-Monkee Michael Nesmith's First National Band. Buddy found himself a job in Ronnie Hawkins's backing band for a while, playing alongside future members of Sea Train and Janis Joplin's Full Tilt Boogie Band, in the Hawks lineup Hawkins assembled to replace the one poached by Dylan for his 1966 tour, which would eventually become The Band. And when folk duo Ian & Sylvia came calling, Buddy took off with them, becoming part of the band that made the legendary *Great Speckled Bird* album in 1969.

It was while touring the following year as part of Great Speckled Bird that Buddy got the biggest break of his career. The group was involved with a huge tour, the Festival Express, that moved en masse through Canada by train, traveling from Toronto to Calgary between June 29 and July 3, 1970. Topping the bill was Janis Joplin, backed by Buddy's old chums from his time with Ronnie Hawkins. Also involved were blues guitarist Buddy Guy, folkies Eric Andersen and Tom Rush, blue-eyed soul ensemble Delaney & Bonnie & Friends, heavy rockers Mountain, and San Francisco legends The Grateful Dead, who had brought along Jerry Garcia's side-project country-rock band New Riders of the Purple Sage as one of the support acts. Effectively, Buddy secured his slot in the New Riders through Garcia's incompetence as a pedal steel guitarist—although to this day, some people still think he was the one who taught Jerry how to play this most complex of instruments.

"Hell no, man!" he snorts dismissively. "If it was me, I would have taught him better! Jeez, I get hung with that a lot! That's just the Grateful Dead rumor mill. Jerry learned all on his own: He got whacked out playing it by himself and needed other people to play with, so he found this guy down in Palo Alto who was doing a little coffee-shop thing playing folk tunes like 'Glendale Train' and 'Garden of Eden,' and Jerry asked if he could sit in with him." The man was songwriter John Dawson, with whom Garcia would found the New Riders as a relaxed, rootsy off-hours alternative to the more intense psychedelic jams that were the Dead's bread and butter. Not that it remained that relaxed for too long.

"As soon as John Dawson said yes, the whole Dead crew moved in and set everything up, and it all started happening," explains Cage. "As soon as people knew Jerry was playing, they wanted to be part of it. Phil Lesh even played bass for a time. This went on for a while until the Dead said, 'Jerry, give it up, man, we gotta go play some shows'—because the Dead was by then a big family machine, with a great payroll that needed to be made through touring, because they weren't selling squat on their albums. Jerry was loath to give up playing pedal steel, so he said, 'Why don't you guys come out with us and be our opener?' which they did for a year or so.

"Then it began getting nuts, because Jerry was just getting wasted and couldn't handle it all. He was so self-conscious about his playing that eventually he told the New Riders, 'You guys have got to get serious and get yourself a real ringer in here, man.'"

The ringer, of course, was just a few compartments down from them on the Festival Express. "As Jerry and Nelson were walking through the stadium one time, they heard me playing and asked me if I wanted to play with them," says Cage. "I had heard The Dead about two years before and walked out of their concert, but by 1970, I couldn't believe what they were doing, and when they asked me to play, it was like there was no rulebook—'Just play it any way you want to. We do!'"

The acquisition of Buddy transformed the New Riders' sound, which became a more confident, driving brand of country rock on their second album (Buddy's first with them), 1972's *Powerglide*. Three years and three albums later, the band was finishing up its *Brujo* album under the watchful eye of the same A&R woman, Ellen Bernstein, who dealt so closely with Bob Dylan.

"She was his A&R out of New York, and then she was flying to California to do work with us," explains Cage. "They started sharing a lot of time together and became very close. I guess we had finished our album before he had his entirely done, and she brought our master out and said to him, 'Look at this, the New Riders are doing one of your tunes'—it was 'You Angel You.' He said, 'Well, can you get me the steel guitar player?'—I suppose it was an afterthought that I could maybe do something with the new tunes he had. So when I got out there, it was brought up: 'Do you want to do these things with Bob? Let's go over and meet Bob at the studio and see what we can get.'"

Which is how, one night late in September 1974, Buddy Cage found himself alone in the vastness of A&R's Studio A, perched over his pedal steel guitar, listening to Bob Dylan's amazing new songs. If working with Dylan wasn't a daunting enough prospect on its own, Buddy was further impressed to find Phil Ramone, probably the hottest producer in the country at that time, working as the engineer.

"The *Blood on the Tracks* session was the first time I met Bob," says Cage. "We went in there, just the three of us, and Bob says, 'Where are the tunes for him, Phil?' Phil just pops it into gear and, like, sixteen, seventeen, or eighteen, some-where in that region, *masterpieces* come out! I was, like, What the fuck!? Dylan says, 'Well, can you do anything? Would you like to start with one?' I said, 'Bob, the best thing I can do to help you is to pack up my guitar and go home.' He said, 'Well, thanks, man, but don't you think you could play on one?' then turns to Phil and says, 'Phil, roll 'em again.'

"Phil played 'em over, and more in exasperation than anything, I said, 'Maybe this one, or that one.' I guess I did about three or four of them—but in any case, 'Meet Me in the Morning' was the one he kept for *Blood on the Tracks*. I was way out in this huge studio that could hold a full or-chestra, a really large room, and I'm in the middle of it—just me, my steel, and my amp. I'd been doing sessions as long as I can remember, and the way I saw it was that Phil was going to run this thing, 'Meet Me in the Morning,' for me and I was going to do a few takes—I usually get the best hits in the first two or three times through. An old Grateful Dead thing is never to stop recording it, and try to record more than you erase; so that was my approach: Let me do it two or three times, and you'll have it—I'm that quick—and he can plug them in wherever he wants, the choices would be up to him and Bob. But that's not what Dylan wanted, apparently: He ended up flashing the light time after time after time, and I found myself having to do six or seven takes."

Worse still, there was little guidance as to what was wrong with the interrupted takes.

"Not only was my wrist getting tired, but there was no conversation, no instructions, no nothing," Cage recalls, "just 'Do it again, do it again.' I was getting really uncomfortable. Then finally the door to the control room opened, and Dylan comes striding out, walks straight up to my steel, and sticks the toes of his cowboy boots under my pedal bar. I don't know why he did that—maybe for emphasis. Anyway, he does that and says, 'The first five verses is singin'— you don't play; the last verse is playin'—you play!' plunks his toes out from under my pedal bar, turns, and strides back into the control room."

During the evening, the control room had begun to fill up with well-wishers and hangers-on, and as the shock over Dylan's rudeness turned into anger at the singer's disrespectful treatment of his instrument, the public humiliation spurred Cage to the brink of rage.

"At that point, in the control room, there was him and Phil Ramone, Mick Jagger, my road manager, my crew chief, my limo driver and bodyguard, and John Hammond, Sr., had come in to hear what I was doing," says Cage, "and at that very instant, for about ten seconds, I was embarrassed to the bone marrow. But as I mentioned before, I was a punk-ass, and that just kicks in; that's always the way it's been with me, and I thought, 'Well, you little fuck, I'm taller than you, and you're not gonna get away with that!' Phil came on the phones then—he was clearly uncomfortable too—and he said, 'You wanna practice one?' and I said, 'No—print it!'

"So the red light came on and I just did one take. I played lightly over the first five verses, but the one where he wanted me to get major was on the verse with 'Look at that sun, sinking like a ship.'"

And get major he did. Fired up with fury, Cage peeled off a searing break that uncoiled through the song's closing stages like an angry snake, providing a piquant counterpoint to the number's relaxed, bluesy tone. Buddy knew he'd nailed it, and without waiting for any further intervention or possible humiliation, he stood up from his instrument with an air of brusque finality.

"I had the picks and the bar off my hands and I was walking away from the guitar before the track was finished, striding into the control room," he recalls. "When I busted into the control room, he was laughin' his ass off! I looked at Ramone, and he was shakin' his head, sayin', 'That was beautiful!' John Hammond said, 'Man, that was unbeliev-able!' I just looked at Dylan and said, 'Fuck you!' and he just laughed—he said, 'Well, we got it!'" The whole thing had been a performance, on both sides of the control room window, Dylan's attitude simply a ruse designed to bring the best out of Cage. A risk, maybe, but one he could afford to take.

"He felt that was the way to get to me, and he broke the ice," says Cage, who instantly realized what Dylan had done. "It was wonderful! I was really grateful."

With that first difficult song out of the way, Buddy quickly completed further overdubs on the strikingly similar "Call Letter Blues," "You're a Big Girl Now," and, he be-lieves, "Tangled Up in Blue." Though none of these ulti-mately made it to the final cut of *Blood on the Tracks*,

"You're a Big Girl Now" eventually appeared on *Biograph,* and "Call Letter Blues" on *The Bootleg Series, Volumes 1–3.*

"I didn't spend a lot of time on them, really," says Buddy. "Like I said in the beginning, 'Bob, these are perfect—what am I going to do with them?' And with that in mind, I think the idea was to keep them minimal—I mean, there was minimal playing on those tracks."

After the session, Cage confides, he joined the others for a drink in the control room, where they had been getting steadily loaded.

"None of us got as drunk as Jagger did, though," laughs Cage. "Mick was in fine form! He kept saying, 'Bob, let me play on a track,' and Bob says, 'No, man, go and sit down.' Mick said, 'Let me play drums or something,' and Bob said, 'You've been dying to play on one of my albums for years now!' We were all laughing, and then Mick just passed out."

With Buddy Cage's overdubs in the can, all that was left was for Paul Griffin, the hugely talented keyboard player whose piano parts, in particular, had contributed so much to the unique character of Dylan's *Highway 61 Revisited* and *Bringing It All Back Home*, to come in and overdub some ghostly breaths of organ on "Idiot Wind." Versions of this evening's work appeared on the test pressing and on *The Bootleg Series, Volumes 1–3.* Griffin, sadly, has since passed away.

Dylan and Phil Ramone reconvened at the studio a few days later, on September 25, to choose the best takes and decide on a track sequence for the album. There were a few decisions to be made between tracks whose melodies were too alike. After Buddy Cage's decisive additions, "Call Letter Blues" was discarded in favor of "Meet Me in the Morning," which was effectively a slower version of the same arrangement with new lyrics, and "Shelter from the Storm" was chosen instead of "Up to Me," whose tune was strikingly similar. It's not hard to see why: With its references to blame, betrayal, and regret, "Up to Me" would just have prolonged the reproachful mood of the album, whereas "Shelter from the Storm" brings a more considered, reflective quality to the song cycle's concluding stages, leading smoothly into the sense of closure imparted by the recently written "Buckets of Rain." "Up to Me" would eventually appear on *Biograph*.

With a running order decided, Ramone prepared a final master of the album and had an acetate cut for Bob to peruse. Having missed out on Dylan's first-ever No. 1 album, Columbia was eager to capitalize on the lingering promotional ripples of *Planet Waves* and the 1974 tour (which had since furnished Asylum with a second hit Dylan album, the live double *Before the Flood*), by getting this new material out in the same year, and work began on packaging and promotion, with the intention of getting it out in two or three weeks.

S I X

BOB DYLAN WAS JUST AS KEEN AS Columbia to release the new album, but the more he listened to the acetate, the less sure he was that this was the way he wanted it to sound. He knew that this was his best batch of material in over half a decade, with the potential to re-establish his reputation as the greatest songwriter of his age, but some songs just weren't being presented to their best advantage. It was largely his own fault, for not coaching the musicians more, and for insisting on inspired immediacy over a more considered recording approach; but in several cases here, the immediacy was rather less than inspired, and the songs seemed to just lie there, inert. He wished there were some way to animate them more, to bring them more vividly to life.

He also started to wonder if some of the songs were too revealing. Always an obsessive tinkerer with lyrics (in many cases, even after the songs had been released), Dylan kept finding better ways to present certain ideas, with more apposite phrasings and evocative images. Some things just seemed a bit corny and embarrassing—that line in "Idiot Wind" about throwing the I Ching, for instance, might come across as a bit too New Agey, and others began to seem too personal. He had always regretted airing his private linen in public in the 1964 song "Ballad in Plain D," which dealt with his breakup with Suze Rotolo, and ever since then he had tried to steer well clear of anything too "confessional," veiling his personal affections and enmities with a screen of metaphor and allusion. But some songs here, particularly "Idiot Wind," might be too readily construed as referring to his crumbling marriage.

So when the usual pre-Christmas workload at the pressing plants caused Columbia to delay the album's manufacture, he seized the opportunity to put the release date back until early in the new year.

"*Blood on the Tracks* was another one of those records we went in and did in three or four days," Dylan explained in the liner notes of *Biograph*. "I had the acetate. I hadn't listened to it for a couple of months. I didn't think I'd got this song off. The record still hadn't come out, and I put it on. I thought the songs could have sounded different, better, so I went in and rerecorded them."

"I think at the time it was possibly just new confusion, having recently moved back to Columbia," reckons Phil Ramone. "They didn't release the record in the two weeks that they had promised to do, which was to get it out rapidly, and I think he had time to sit around, and once you do that you reflect, and then you worry, and then typically, you add strings, horns, anything . . ."

Dylan was not of a mind to try and cover up the songs' shortcomings by smothering them in strings and horns. He knew the problems were more fundamental than that, that some of them required a complete overhaul. His suspicions were confirmed that December when he returned to the Crow River Farm for the holidays and played the acetate for his younger brother, David Zimmerman. David, a producer of radio and TV jingles and manager of local singer-song-writing talent, reportedly told him that the recording lacked commercial appeal and might not attract radio airplay in its current state.

But, he added, it wasn't completely unsalvageable: Why didn't Bob let him make a few discreet calls and try to sort something out? David's response would have a decisive effect on the final version of *Blood on the Tracks* and would also constitute a watershed moment in the relations between the two brothers.

■   ■   ■

Most of Bob Dylan's biographers document a playful, active childhood in Hibbing, Minnesota. Bobby and his younger brother, David Zimmerman, born five years apart (Bobby in 1941, David in 1946), grew up under the watchful eye of their father, Abraham, and the loving care and unbridled adoration of the one woman who would remain closest to Bob throughout her life, his beloved mother, Beatrice "Beatty" Zimmerman.

The family had relocated from Duluth in 1947 following Abe's debilitating bout with polio. Living first in an apartment, then in a modest home near an abandoned open-pit iron mine, the boys were well liked by friends and neighbors. An elderly woman who knew them well in Hibbing remembers David as "The Little Rabbi," more interested in his Bible studies than was his older, more worldly brother, who pursued an early penchant for country music, rhythm and blues, and rock 'n' roll, his hunger fed by a handful of eclectic fifty-thousand-watt clear-channel radio stations dotting the American South, which beamed powerfully into the magnetic plains of the Mesabi Range of northern Minnesota.

The Mesabi in winter is desolate and frozen, and the isolation it brings can easily trigger an internal search for meaning. So the young Bobby Zimmerman would eagerly scan the family radio dial after dark, in search of new worlds beyond Hibbing. The music varied greatly, and his early influences came from all quarters.

"We liked Gene Vincent," Bob's childhood chum John Bucklen told journalist Dave Engels of *On the Tracks* magazine. "We bought some of those blue caps like he had, with a little visor that snaps on and off. Bob bought an album. We took it to his bedroom, put it on, and air-guitared along with it. Then we saw his dad, standing in the doorway staring at us. That kind of blew the whole thing. His dad kind of shook his head and said, 'What the hell you doing?' It was embarrassing."

Even back then, Bob had developed the cruel streak that would burst out so spectacularly later on in songs such as "Positively 4th Street."

"He was a master of the put-on," recalled Bucklen. "I just remember his laughter and him saying to me, 'Sing something,' and when I did, he said, 'Damn, you're good. That kid's really good!' I started to believe him. He was playing a joke with me. And he hasn't changed. He was a bit cruel. There was a current of hostility, or whatever. After that one encounter with him, I caught on to what he was doing and kind of resented him for it. I thought, 'Who needs him?' I didn't care—I had other friends."

For all his desire to perform in high school rock 'n' roll combos, Bobby was known as a shy and somewhat introverted youth among his classmates; yet he fit into a classic "big brother" role at home in his dealings with David, whom he dominated through childhood and adolescence. According to friends and colleagues, that essential chemistry between the brothers intensified as they became adults, defining their relationship for years to come.

One doesn't have to search too far for evidence of the inevitability of sibling rivalry, particularly between brothers. The field of pop music alone is littered with the spite and bitterness of broken families. Don and Phil Everly, most famously, hated each other with a passion that precluded their speaking to each other offstage, and that eventually split their creative partnership. Ray and Dave Davies of The Kinks regularly came to blows onstage, assaulting each other with guitars, cymbals, and whatever else came to hand. And more recently, Noel and Liam Gallagher of Britpop band Oasis seem to like nothing more than giving one another a fat lip just for looking funny at the other—which in their case is, admittedly, hard to avoid. So although David Zimmerman did eventually make a career in the music industry, it's perhaps just as well that he didn't try to compete with his brother on a national or global level but remained content to serve as manager and producer of local acts in the Minneapolis area.

As it was, their youthful relationship was marked by the kind of commonplace malice and mischief with which all older brothers exercise their dominance over younger siblings. One of Bobby's favorite taunts involved stationing twelve-year-old David in the driveway at their modest home at 2425 Seventh Avenue in Hibbing and entreating him to stay in place while he rode his first motorcycle out into the street and back, gunning straight toward the hapless David, who would stand petrified in the center of the drive, trusting only that his brother would not kill him.

It was a trust based more on filial faith and blind hope than experience, given Bob's questionable biking skills. John Bucklen, with whom he would sometimes ride, remembers well one time when Bob almost got himself run over by a train at a railroad crossing.

"It was a double track," Bucklen recalls. "There was a long train going by. We're sitting there gunning our cycles, getting kind of antsy. The train goes by, and he guns it to take off. Just as he guns it, the main warning signal goes off. He takes off first—a train's coming from the opposite direction! Bob goes forward and slides sideways, almost under the wheels of the train. I remember the guy in the train sticking his head out the window, looking.

"The train goes by. Bob picks up his cycle and pushes it across the track. I remember him getting off his cycle and putting his head down like this. It's just a knee-jerk reaction. He was obviously shook up. He was a terrible driver. . . . He just didn't handle the thing that well."

On another occasion, Bob ran into a three-year-old boy who darted out between parked cars, chasing an orange. Luckily, the child sustained no lasting injuries. All Bob could remember, he told his girlfriend Echo Helstrom, was the orange rolling across the street. Fortunately, there was never an accident with Bob's own kin, either. He would stop inches from David's frame, screeching on the brakes just in the nick of time, and roaring with laughter at his prank, which just got funnier each time David submitted to it.

"David didn't like it so much," says photographer Nancy Bundt, whom David told about Bob's pranks in the '70s. "If his brother put that much pressure on him when he was twelve, to stand there while he almost killed him with a motorcycle, can you imagine the pressure Bob put on him as an adult to protect his interests? I think David was a nice guy, a regular kind of guy."

"He's a nice guy," affirms Ellen Steinman, who supervised and managed David Zimmerman's local business interests for ten years. "You have to understand that he's not a perfect person; he's got his own life that he built, being in Bob's shadow, with all of the choices he's made in his life. David was always working when Bob was here. Nobody ever said to David, 'You're not supposed to be in a relationship like that; you're supposed to be *family*.' It's apparent from the outside that Bob's success had a huge effect on David."

No mystery surrounds the perceived threat and devastation for an older child suddenly joined by a younger sibling—particularly in the competitive, aspirational atmosphere of a typical Jewish-American family.

"The firstborn is deified by the mother," explains Rabbi Sim Glaser of Temple Israel in Minneapolis. "He is the God, and then his brother comes along and usurps his throne. And so forever, he has been ripped down from this notion of being the only one, the cherished one. You never quite get over being dethroned, having your mother taken away from you, and having to share her with others. Many firstborn Jewish men go into the clergy, because all these women are going to set them up for adoration again. All these firstborns that came along thought they were going to be God, and then another little boy comes along after them and says, 'No, you're not so great, there is only one great being in the world and that is God.' One brother thinks he's God, and the other has a relationship with the God. It's hard for firstborns to have a relationship with God. We think we *are* God!"

Beatty Zimmerman did little to dispel this notion while enjoying a Dylan concert from a private box at Minneapolis's Metrodome, gushing proudly, "Look at Bob! Look at this place! He is God, and everybody's here to worship him!" Ellen Steinman, who overheard the comment, thought it strange: "It's hard to not put Bob up there, ratchet him up a little bit; it's just human nature. But it's a pretty weird thing to say, you know?"

"Bob was likely deified by his mother during the first four years of his life," speculates Rabbi Glaser. "And that's how people like that are made, by mothers who tell their kids that everything they do is wonderful. So then this other kid comes along and obviously he's going to despise him, even if the younger brother doesn't seem to be amounting to anything nearly as great as Dylan is going to be in a few short years. He's still the younger brother, he's still a threat, and so he goes nuts on him."

John Bucklen confirms the decisive influence of Beatty Zimmerman on the young Bob.

"I got to know her a little bit," he explains. "So friendly—she was always asking, concerned about you, 'How you doin'?' I really didn't mind visiting Bob, because she was nice, except on the other hand there was his father, who was very stoic, always looked at you kind of 'What the hell are *you* doing here?' That's the feeling I got . . . I'm sure he got along fine with his mother, but not so well with his dad."

But as Bucklen told biographer Howard Sounes, there was little interaction between Bob and his brother.

"I don't recall him having a very warm, friendly discussion with David," he said. "David was just his little brother. And David was so radically different from Bob in his personality. He was probably the type of kid that any parent would like to raise—he was studious, and wasn't wild at all."

In her book *Mixed Feelings: Love, Hate, Rivalry and Reconciliation Among Brothers and Sisters,* Francine Klagsbrun illustrates how birth order can affect sibling relationships. "In childhood, the simple reality of having been born first bears with it every expectation of remaining first," she explains. "Because so much of the identity of the older gets built around this expectation of superiority, a reversal of positions can threaten the very foundation of the older's self-view. Many younger siblings continue throughout life to admire elder brothers *and* resent them, seek their protection *and* reject it, strive to outstrip them *and* fear outstripping them. No matter how they behave toward others, in relation to their older brothers, they continue to behave as younger siblings."

Rabbi Glaser concurs with Klagsbrun's analysis. "Historically, the younger brother always in some ways adores that older brother, even if he hates him," he says. "If he's angry at his brother for something, or his brother mistreated him as a child, he's going to want to get up and say, 'I'm going to compete with you!' And that's not only because he's second to a giant; it's also because he must have had some bad vibes with his brother."

Rabbi Glaser illustrates this dichotomy by recourse to Talmudic scholarship.

"There are a number of brothers throughout biblical history, none of whom got along," he explains. "The first ones were Cain and Abel, Jacob and Esau. There's also Isaac and Ishmael—imagery which Dylan uses in 'Highway 61 Revisited.' In Jewish tradition, the older brother is supposed to be the inheritor, called the *bahur*. In every one of those stories, something terrible happens: The firstborn is the one who goes out there and makes the mistakes, and everybody else kind of learns from that. It's not about material; it's more about intellect, and maturity, and morality. The older brothers aren't necessarily the most moral; they go through much of their lives trying to prove something.

"So, in the case of Bobby and David, when 1974 rolls around, you have a moment where Bob Dylan is at a low point, and he doesn't know where to turn; and all of a sudden, his little brother is speaking to him about something, and he listens. David forgives Bob at that point for the motorcycle taunting and the way he was treated, and says, 'I'm going to help you, big brother.' That's tenderness on his part. Bob has also grown up, and at that moment he doesn't need the adoration of the masses—he needs *help*. So when his younger brother helps him, offers him advice, he thinks, 'You may be right—thank you, little brother.' It's a moment of tenderness. He couldn't have done that ten or twenty years earlier, because he was still playing out the psychodynamic problems of having a younger brother who usurped him."

"It's very biblical," believes Rabbi Glaser, offering as precedent the story of Jacob and Esau, in which Jacob steals his older brother's birthright and fears Esau will kill him if they meet again. Later, after being persuaded by an angel to be a mensch and confront the situation, Jacob goes out to meet Esau, each of them accompanied by huge armies. "Esau goes out, runs over to his brother, grabs him by the head and gives him a violent kiss on his neck. A violent kiss, which is a combination of intense, lifelong anger and his love of his brother, which can never die. It's the ultimate ambivalence. He is pulled in two ways, and that's where these two guys were in 1974. They love each other, but they hate each other, and that's brothers for you."

Such, perhaps, was the nature of Bob and David's reconciliation, a realization on the part of both men that, contrary to received wisdom, you *are* your brother's keeper, whatever disputes may have pulled you apart. Interestingly, the nature of sibling relationships has a peculiar distinction in Talmudic scholarship, as Glaser explains.

"There's something that only happens in one place in the Torah," he says. "All it says in the English is 'Esau went ahead, bowed low seven times until he was near his brother. Esau ran to his brother; he kissed him'—but if you look at the Hebrew, it is the only place in the whole Torah, *vayishakayu*, where you have dots on every single syllable on the top of a word like this, which signify emphasis, because you're supposed to say the word violently. He was angry at his younger brother, but he needed him at that moment, and he loved him—in Hebrew it says all this; it says everything about that moment."

And so the brothers conferred over Christmas, coming up with a plan so far-fetched and improbable only Bob Dylan could ever pull it off. But not without his brother.

David's moment had arrived.

Bob Dylan live, on tour with The Band, January 4, 1974, nearly a year before recording *Blood on the Tracks* but the same week the album's cover photo was taken in Toronto by Ron Coro. Photo by Jeff Klein.

"The Farm" in Minnesota where Bob Dylan has spent many summers since 1974 and where many of the songs on *Blood on the Tracks* were written in a red notebook. The converted barn to the right is Bob's house.

Phil Ramone, who produced the New York sessions of *Blood on the Tracks*. Courtesy of Phil Ramone.

Deliverance, 1975, one year after the *Blood on the Tracks* sessions. Back: John Crowder, bass; Richard Crooks, drums; Kenny Kosek, fiddle. Front: Charlie Brown, electric guitar; Eric Weissberg, leader, steel guitar, banjo, guitar, dobro. Courtesy of Eric Weissberg.

David Zimmerman and Kevin Odegard in front of the Orpheum Theater, Minneapolis. Photo by Barbara P. Odegard.

Chris Weber with Dylan's 1934 0042G Martin, immediately prior to delivery, 1974. Photo by Jeff Klein.

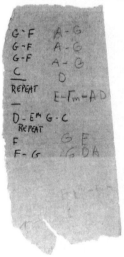

Dylan's handwritten chart for "Tangled Up In Blue." Courtesy of Sam Seiden.

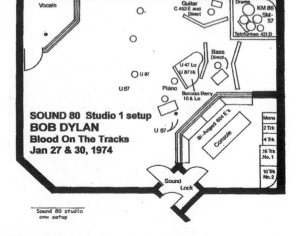

Sound 80 Studio 1 setup for *Blood on the Tracks*. Courtesy of Herb Pilhofer.

Bill Berg's illustration of the only rehearsal for "Lily, Rosemary and the Jack of Hearts." Courtesy of Bill Berg.

"Lily, Rosemary and the Jack of Hearts," Take One. Illustration by Bill Berg.

Paul Martinson, 1974. Courtesy of Herb Pilhofer.

Bill Berg, 1974. Courtesy of Herb Pilhofer.

David Zimmerman portrait, striking a familiar profile. Photo by Nancy Bundt.

Billy Peterson. Courtesy of Willard O. Peterson.

Peter Ostroushko. Courtesy
of Peter Ostroushko.

Gregg Inhofer. Courtesy
of Gregg Inhofer.

Tony Brown. Courtesy
of Tony Brown.

Dylan live, January 1974, Chicago Stadium. Photo by Jeff Klein.

SEVEN

WINTER CUTS HARD THROUGH MINNEAPOLIS, a place so cold that the city installed the famous "Skyway" system of enclosed walkways to enable shoppers to cross city-center streets without having to brave the ten- to twenty-below blasts of ice-flecked wind. Take a walk outdoors, and the wind will freeze before it reaches your throat. It's *that* cold. Let's just say that even Chicagoans consider Minneapolis chilly.

So when the phone rang one particularly crisp and blustery night just after Christmas 1974 in Kevin Odegard and Joe Stanger's apartment overlooking the southeast rail yards, they ignored it and carried on watching a *Kojak* rerun on TV. The flatmates were brakemen on the Chicago & Northwestern Railroad, and they knew it would be the crew dispatcher calling them in to work. And who wanted to ride the "big iron" in this weather?

Only on the umpteenth ring did Odegard relent and pick up the receiver. As it happened, it wasn't the railroad calling after all.

On the line was David Zimmerman, asking where he could find a guitar for his brother. A very specific guitar: a rare 1937 0042 Martin, the compact, small-bodied acoustic known in folk music circles as the "Joan Baez" model, because of her long-term patronage of it. A twenty-four-year-old part-time musician, Odegard had once been managed by Zimmerman, a local record producer, and knew him quite well; tonight, his voice had a special urgency to it. Odegard quickly found out why. David's brother, Bob—better known to the world as Bob Dylan—was in town, and Bob was looking for that rare and precious instrument.

"I can make some calls and see what's out there," said Odegard. He hung up, dialed a familiar number, and as luck would have it, hit pay dirt right away. Chris Weber had a guitar that closely fit this description at his Dinkytown music shop, The Podium. Not many local musicians, however, would have need for such an instrument—not to mention the funds necessary to purchase it. Weber's interest was piqued.

"What do you need it for?" he asked.

"I can't really tell you right now, but I'll call back later with details," replied Odegard, adding cryptically, "I might have a buyer for it, but I don't have permission to talk about it yet."

"Okay," said Chris and hung up his phone. Such intrigue! What was all this about? And who could this mysterious potential purchaser be?

"When Kevin called the first time," recalls Weber, "the guitar was seven feet away from me! I had just taken it in on consignment two or three days earlier. We had a section of the store that was specifically devoted to used guitars, and there were a lot of regulars who used to come through and check 'em out, 'cause every week there were a couple of new ones. Kevin called the first time and asked about it, and I thought, well, this was a very special guitar you weren't going to find anywhere, and he asked specifically for that guitar. So I thought at first that he had already been down and seen it when I wasn't there, and he was angling to begin a haggling session with me, which was typical of the guitar business. When he asked for that vintage and model, I thought, well, he's obviously seen the guitar. It was only after the second phone call I realized that he had not seen it, and that he was pleasantly surprised to hear that I had such an item."

Though not quite the exact model Odegard had inquired about, the guitar Weber had in stock was, as the saying goes, close enough for jazz.

"Actually, it was a 1934 0042G," says Weber. "The G means gut-string model setup, so it wasn't exactly the guitar Bob requested. The neck was a little bit wider, and it wasn't really designed for steel strings, although it was strong enough to support them. It was certainly close enough and was an instrument that I knew he would appreciate and that he might like. He did eventually buy it.

"Joan Baez was the first performer on the scene to have that be her main instrument for performing and recording. Back in those days, a smaller-bodied acoustic guitar was a better recording instrument because it had fewer overtones, and so it got cleaner sound through the big tube Neumann microphones. Plus she's a woman and it's smaller, easier to handle, and so it became the instrument of choice. My guess is that the Woody Guthrie guitars were probably small-body guitars, too. [Big-bodied] Dreadnoughts really only came into being in the late '30s, so smaller-bodied guitars were the guitar of choice."

Kevin relayed the good news to David, who stunned Odegard with his next request.

"Can you help me line up some musicians?" asked Zimmerman. "Bobby's not happy with his new record and wants to redo a song or two at Sound 80."

While Joe Stanger sat obliviously in front of the television waiting for the railroad dispatcher to send him out into the snowy night, David and Kevin mulled over a lineup of musicians who would be ideal for the sessions. David listened patiently while Odegard lobbied for his pals Stanley Kipper and Doug Nelson to sit in on drums and fretless bass. But David had already made up his mind: His first and only choice for this critical assignment was the "house" rhythm section at Sound 80 Studio, with whom he was familiar and comfortable.

Billy Peterson and Bill Berg were an inspired choice as bassist and drummer, respectively. Well trained, and working as jazz and improvisational musicians with their fusion band Natural Life, they were among the nation's finest players and certainly of a caliber second to none in the local area. Berg also happened to be a Hibbing native who'd graduated from high school with David in 1964 and had first encountered Dylan before he was Dylan.

"My dad, who was a jazz piano player in Hibbing, took me to see the Golden Chords play at the St. Louis County Fairgrounds Grandstand in about 1959," recalls Berg. "My classmate's brother, Bobby Zimmerman, was playing in that group at the time. Although we grew up in Hibbing, that was the first time I had seen Bobby play live music." Even at such an early stage of his musical career, the singer made a big impression on the youngster. "I had seen and heard about Buddy Holly and Bobby Vee at the time, but I wasn't quite into the things Bobby was doing," acknowledges Berg. "He was way ahead of his time, even then."

Like Berg, Billy Peterson's father was a jazz pianist—as, indeed, was his mother. Between them, they lured young Billy into music by simply leaving instruments lying around the house and letting him discover them for himself. By his teens, Billy was proficient enough on drums, piano, and bass to play drums on some of his dad's dates—particularly the Mormon gigs, at which there would be no danger of the youngster being exposed to the usual high-octane, boozy lifestyle endured by club musicians—and was already being taught the rudiments of harmony by his mother. Drawn to the bass, Peterson taught himself runs by slowing down guitarist Pat Martino's records, which effectively transposed the guitar licks into the bass register. By 1963, he was out touring the Midwest with The Righteous Brothers, who had just had a Top 50 hit with "Little Latin Lupe Lu" and were about to be propelled into history by Phil Spector. He would spend the rest of the decade developing his skills both on the road and on studio dates, using Minneapolis as his base.

By the early '70s, Berg and Peterson had become the region's premier rhythm section, noted for their flexibility and inventiveness. Despite their personal preference for jazz, they could turn their hand to just about any style and had recently demonstrated a particular sensitivity to the needs of acoustic folk musicians. Immediately before their work on *Blood on the Tracks*, Berg had played on Cat Stevens's *Buddha and the Chocolate Box*—a Top 3 album earlier that year—and both players had developed a close musical relationship with cult folk-guitar legend Leo Kottke, with whom they had just recorded the *Dreams and All That Stuff* album at Sound 80.

"Leo Kottke put us into the frame of mind of what we play and what we did *not* play being equally important," explains Berg. "When to lay back and let the lead man do his thing—especially Leo, who was not the most verbal virtuoso in the business, but just an amazing talent. We didn't know, and neither did he, how he played as well as he did, but we did learn to support him in a way that seemed to work. That was the best training Billy Peterson and I had for the Dylan sessions. Leo Kottke taught us everything we needed to know without saying a word."

"Working with Kottke was the ideal preparation for the Dylan session," agrees Peterson. "Leo would move like Muhammad Ali on the ropes—you never knew what he was going to do with his guitar! He was always there ahead of you, so you were hung out to dry, but Berg was always burning right there with him. And Berg is a genius on the drums. The more you throw at him the better he reacts. He is so quick to react in any changing circumstance, and the more it would change, the more creative he could be. You just can't throw him off: He just gets better, especially on the rebound. He recovers with moves that give the music a whole new life."

David Zimmerman's insistence on hiring Berg and Peterson ultimately proved to be the single most crucial factor in the success of the sessions.

"I would say Berg and Peterson were Dylan's primary creative foils on the project," concedes Kevin Odegard. "They provided the synergy that made that record great."

On keyboards, David and Kevin agreed to invite Kevin's recent find, fusion whiz kid Gregg Inhofer, to the proceedings.

"Kevin gave me a call one day and said, 'Hey, David wants you to play on a Dylan session this Friday,'" says Inhofer. "I said, 'Wow, great,' and I showed up. I wasn't starstruck, because I wasn't that big of a Dylan fan. I appreciated what he did at the time, and I respected it, but it wasn't like I sat at home and listened to Dylan records over and over in my spare time. I was listening to John McLaughlin and things like that."

The session lineup was just about settled. But in the volley of invitations and negotiations that ensued, David Zimmerman reluctantly agreed to have Chris Weber—who was keen to protect his valuable guitar, and hopeful to close a sale—tag along to the session.

"Kevin kept calling back and finally got the okay from David to present the instrument to Bob," recalls Weber. "That was cute, and the secrecy factor was funny. Kevin made me promise him I wouldn't tell a soul! He said, 'Here's the deal: It's for Bob Dylan. Why don't you show up at my apartment at five o'clock, and maybe you'll get to meet him, and who knows, maybe he'll buy the guitar.' So that was the premise for me showing up at Kevin's place and waiting. When it was time to go, we simply got in the car and started driving toward the studio. That's when Kevin revealed that we were apparently going to a studio to record something."

The session was to take place at Sound 80 Studio, a state-of-the-art facility with a reputation among local musicians as "the best room in town." Located between an old working-class neighborhood and a light industrial section of South Minneapolis, near the Mississippi River, it stood anonymously among the houses and parking lots at the corner of Twenty-seventh Street and Twenty-fifth Avenue South. With a trolley-car diner next door and Skol Liquors directly across the street, it was the perfect location for a lonely superstar in search of a hideout.

Paul Martinson was the engineer at Sound 80, where he had made four records with renowned guitarist Leo Kottke. He was not restricted to folk music alone, however, having previously spent several years at Empire Photo Sound working on industrial movies, recording dialogue and narration, and doing some location work. At Sound 80, Martinson had learned the nuts and bolts of music recording from the studio's two engineers, Tom Jung and Scott Rivard. "All of my initial training on how to use the rooms and baffles and so on was from Tom," he says. "From Scott I learned about circuits and tape heads, tape transports, and electronics." He soon became adept at recording any size band, from small combos to full choirs, demonstrating his versatility with sessions for both the Minnesota Orchestra and the St. Paul Chamber Orchestra.

"We recorded everything from classical music, all the way through pop and rock, down to local polka bands and school choirs," he affirms. "We recorded everything! Including quite a bit of work for radio and television commercials. Northwest Airlines was our biggest commercial client—we were the keepers of the official Northwest 'gong' you heard in the commercials for Northwest Orient, as it was known then. First Bank (now US Bank), Norwest Bank (Wells Fargo), Dayton-Hudson (now Marshall Field/Target), 3M, Pillsbury, General Mills: They were all clients."

He had also worked on two or three projects before with David Zimmerman, including an album by Kevin Odegard, so when Zimmerman called him on December 26, he was not surprised—until he learned who was involved in the session.

"David told me that Bob was going to record some songs at Sound 80," recalls Martinson. "He didn't say how many—at least one or two. We talked about a drummer and a bass player, and we both liked Bill Berg and Billy Peterson—there was no reason to discuss anything else in terms of a rhythm section. Berg and Peterson were not just the core of the Sound 80 rhythm section that we used for all of our projects; they were widely appreciated in the entire music community and played in any number of configurations around town, in all idioms, which was mirrored in their studio work. They played with many, many different people at the studio. We'd have a gospel group, with two guitar players—in would come Berg and Peterson. And they played jazz, pop, jingles, rock—everything. So when they came in and Kevin, Chris, and Gregg were there, they could feel right at home, as long as the other players were good musicians and playing in tune. They weren't elitist at all. They were just very comfortable playing with other good players."

For a while, however, it seemed as though Berg, at least, would not be playing on the session. He had become disenchanted with the Minneapolis music scene, and his thoughts, at that point in his life, were thousands of miles away, in Los Angeles.

"My ambivalence about Minneapolis came about from feeling that we'd done everything we could do with the fusion band," he explains. "A complacency began to settle in, and I set my sights on a career as a musician in Southern California."

By Christmas, Berg was packed and ready to roll. His white Volvo station wagon was stuffed with most of his worldly possessions, and a trailer hitched behind contained his record collection and all of his musical gear. "I was very excited to be leaving for Los Angeles, having tentatively lined up living quarters near the beach in Venice," Berg recalls. "Then just after Christmas, the telephone rang, and it was the Zelenovich office, which at that time lined up much of the jingle and session work I was doing with Billy Peterson. David Zimmerman worked out of that office, along with Mark Zelenovich, Sr., with whom he was very close friends. We were told Bob Dylan was in town, and that he might want to record, but we were really led to believe that it was just going to be some sort of a demo session, maybe to try out new songs, or whatever.

"I actually deliberated for a while, then decided it would be a good thing to do and delayed my departure to Los Angeles to show up and try this thing out with Billy. Still, it definitely didn't feel like the real McCoy at that point, just a good session opportunity. There was no pressure; it was not at all unlike the Leo Kottke stuff Billy and I had been doing recently, so we went in fairly relaxed about it—at least, I did. I don't think they even told Billy it was a Dylan session! Just told him to show up—because he was mighty surprised to see Dylan there when he arrived to tune up his new cherry-red electric bass."

"David Zimmerman just called on Thursday and said, 'Billy, show up at Sound 80 tomorrow night,'" recalls Peterson. "He didn't tell me what it was for—I assumed it was another ad or jingle."

The session was set for the following evening, Friday, December 27, when there was little, if any, other activity at the studio. Paul Martinson had a sense of destiny about this project.

"I felt that I had been chosen by David to do this because he and I had done a number of things before, so I knew that he had confidence in me," he says. "Knowing Kevin and Gregg, and having worked a lot with Peterson and Berg, I was able to go into it with reasonable confidence. Although the fact that I had no one to help me set up around the holidays made me a little concerned. Before that first session on Friday night, I asked Scott Rivard to work with me to make sure I had everything for the session—he remains one of the finest technical recording people in the country and is now the sound engineer on Garrison Keillor's *Prairie Home Companion*. But he had to leave, and although I would like to have had an assistant, I also figured that once we had set up the session, I wouldn't have to change very much because it would stay the same, both players and equipment."

While Martinson was busy setting up the various microphones and baffles for the session, the musicians began arriving, understandably nervous with anticipation. When Billy Peterson arrived and saw Bob Dylan in the studio, he shot a few fleeting looks around the room, muttered, "What the hell's goin' on?" under his breath, and chuckled, before charging into the session with a ferocious, contagious intensity.

It wasn't the first time that Kevin Odegard had worked for Dylan. Wary about the way his earlier demos and outtakes were appearing on bootlegs, Bob had, through his brother, hired Kevin to record some of his new songs as publishing demos a year or two before, correctly surmising that Odegard was less likely to be bootlegged than himself.

"I was one musician who was asked to record material so Bob could shop the publishing on the songs and try to get country artists or other artists to record them," explains Odegard. "I was hired to record a song I remember as 'Nobody 'Cept You,' which can now be found in folios. I remember he had [Tex-Mex country star] Johnny Rodriguez in mind for that one."

Accordingly, Odegard was less awed than the others at meeting Dylan—though even he was nervous at the prospect of actually recording with him.

"Dylan was kind and chatty, comfortable to be with, friendly, engaging—all the things you don't associate with Bob Dylan," he recalls.

To the others, the living legend initially seemed shy and reserved.

"When Dylan appeared at the session," says Gregg Inhofer, "he had a cold. He just wanted to get it over with. He was pretty wrapped up in his coat, sat by himself, and didn't really say a lot to anybody unless they spoke to him."

"At the beginning of the first session, he settled in slowly," agrees Martinson. "While the others finished setting up, and we were doing a couple of mikes, he sat by himself and read a newspaper. David talked to him a little bit, as did Chris and Kevin, who knew him a little. But once we started doing the music, he seemed to settle down and talked to the other musicians. I think he basically was just very shy at the beginning. Then once he got the sense that it was gonna work, and that the session was going well, he relaxed."

Chris Weber helped break the ice by jumping in with both feet and showing Dylan the Martin guitar he had brought in for him.

"We went over to the corner of the studio, and he began to look at the guitar and strum it," he recalls. "The drums were being set up by this time, and there was a lot of noise from the other instruments. Right next to us was this corner glass vocal recording booth, about the size of two phone booths, with two chairs and a music stand and a microphone. I suggested that we could go in there and we would be able to hear the instrument, so we went in there with the guitar I was hoping to sell him and sat down. We chatted for five or ten minutes. He asked me if I played, and whether I wrote anything. I said sure, and he said 'Well, play me something you wrote.'

"I played a song that I wrote called '"A" Rag,' a nice little light finger-picking-style instrumental, and he said, 'Wow, you play well,' and I thanked him and said that I'd been playing all my life. Dylan said, 'Do you write any words?' Sheepishly, I said yes. Here I was, going to sing my modest lyrics to the spokesman of our generation! He said, 'Well, sing me something with words.' So I sang him a love song called 'Come on Home with Me' that I had written. He sat patiently for three minutes and listened to me while I played this song, and when I finished he said, 'That's a nice tune; Ronstadt should do that.' And I thought to myself, 'That's wonderful, Bob, maybe you could make that happen'—but he didn't say anything, of course!"

Then Bob said, "Here's one of mine," and began playing a new tune. To the other musicians, it sounded oddly disconcerting.

"He started off with a C minor chord, then went rather dissonant," says Odegard. "It sounded all wrong at first, then gradually, as he went through it, you understood there was a pattern to it, and that it did work."

The song was "Idiot Wind," Dylan's most damning putdown song since such wrathful '60s anthems as "Like a Rolling Stone" and "Positively 4th Street." Evidently satisfied with the guitarist's abilities, Dylan coopted Chris Weber as a kind of musical go-between, to convey the song's structure to the others.

"He must have had enough confidence in my playing that he asked me if I would learn a song and teach it to the bass player, drummer, and keyboard player," says Weber, "because he wanted to keep it fresh and didn't want to have to keep going over it. So he laid down a C minor chord, asked me the name of the chord, and I identified it as a C minor; he said, 'Yup, that's where it starts.' He proceeded to teach me the progression of the song 'Idiot Wind,' which I had not heard—and no one else had heard, to the best of my knowledge. In a few minutes we worked out the song. I suggested an A minor seventh chord instead of the A seventh chord that he had been playing, and he said, 'Leave that in there; that sounds nice.' I learned the song, we left the booth, and I went out and taught it to the band."

"Chris was a good go-between with Bob and us, although Bob did loosen up later," says Peterson. "Chris came out of the booth after working with Bob and sat over with us in the far corner and showed 'Idiot Wind' to us, and of course, boom, Berg had it instantly. He hears a tune like that one time through and he's dialed into it, y'know? He said, 'Oh, I know what I'm going to do on this.' I jotted a quick chord chart out myself for that one. We developed that song as the takes went by and went fairly deep into the takes before we got one."

While the band was rehearsing the song, Dylan and his young son, Jakob, adjourned to the vending machines down the hall to get some coffee. Once Martinson had the microphones correctly set up and Peterson's new prototype Les Paul solid-body electric double bass directly injected via a transformer into the mixing console, Weber came out to tell Bob the band was ready, and they returned to the studio.

"Dylan walked straight into the vocal booth," says Weber. "There was no guitar set-up in the main room: Everything was baffled off for the bass, drums, and keyboard, and I was a fifth wheel. I hung on to the guitar, figuring maybe I could just sit in the control booth, hang around and listen to the recording session, and he gave me a puzzled look through the glass of the corner booth. I went over and asked if I could stay and listen from the control booth, and he said, 'No, man, I need you to play guitar.' I got extremely excited! I'd had no idea that was coming, there was no indication. So I just picked up and played the 1934 0042 on 'Idiot Wind.'"

Dylan led the charge, thundering into the first live band and vocal take.

"He was kinda reticent about it at first," recalls Paul Martinson, who was recording the proceedings on a 15ips (inches per second) Ampex 300 mastering deck. "But once we got into the first song, which was 'Idiot Wind,' the bass player and drummer immediately got onto the tune with the keyboard player, and things just kinda moved along from there."

"It was breathtaking and beautiful at the same time," says Odegard. "The song was a striking throwback to an earlier Dylan sound, circa 1965, and it was like the snarling, spitting Dylan of a decade earlier was in the room with us, throwing an agonizing poetic tantrum. It took quite a few takes, that first song, maybe five or six takes, mostly because Paul, who was alone, wasn't quite ready with the studio set-up. But Dylan kept the freshness about that one, and it has a very different feel from the New York session version—it bears a closer resemblance to, say, the '60s work than to anything he's done since, particularly with the organ. He overdubbed that organ himself, in fact: He knew what he was going for, how he wanted it to sound—he turned on the Leslie speaker and overdubbed it.

"You can hear a lot of Dylan overdubbing on the Minneapolis sessions: He overdubbed on every single song—he even overdubbed a mandolin on 'If You See Her, Say Hello,' borrowed it from Peter Ostroushko to play what's called a 'butterfly' part, in a higher register; Peter played his part, but Dylan played it as well. And Dylan overdubbed the flamenco guitar parts on 'You're a Big Girl Now' and 'If You See Her, Say Hello,' too."

In the control booth, Paul Martinson was busy trying to achieve the right tone and balance between the various instruments and Dylan's impassioned vocal. After a few takes, he had achieved what he considered an optimum rough mix.

"At Sound 80, we were taught to start mixing immediately on the first run-through," he explains, "because ultimately it would always lead to a much better product. And also because we did many sessions where the meter was running: The small band from Wahpeton, North Dakota, say, that had come into town to record two tunes, only had an hour and a half in the studio, so you mixed straight to two-track, got their two songs down, and handed them to the mastering engineer. I also know that the musicians appreciated it because they didn't have to put up with my fiddling around trying to get an overall mix. We would immediately have a good comprehensive mix, and as the session went on, you could fine-tune the mix from there and adjust your equalization and compressor settings. We recorded so much stuff live, you'd have to come up with strong early mixes.

"That was our training, and it paid off. At an early playback, Bob—who was in a separate booth—came into the control room and listened to the playback and made the comment to me, 'You have a nice way of picking things up here.' Which, of course, made me relax right away and think, 'Oh good, he likes it; we're gonna do some pretty good work here.'"

After Dylan had "punched in" a few vocals on "Idiot Wind," bassist Billy Peterson had to leave to play his regular (prearranged) gig at a local jazz club. "The band had my heart and soul," he explains. "The thing with Dylan was cool and I loved it and really appreciated being a part of it, but leaving the session was not hard because I had to get to work. These jazz heads in my band didn't care about me recording with Bob Dylan—the be-boppers didn't understand Bob Dylan. Especially Bob Rockwell, the great tenor sax player. He said, 'I don't give a shit *who* you're recording with.'" With Peterson gone, the rest of the musicians figured they were done for the night.

"We were just hanging around listening to what we had done," recalls Chris Weber, "when Paul Martinson came over to me and said that Dylan wanted to do something else. So we went over in the corner again and he taught me 'You're a Big Girl Now.' That song has that same Martin guitar on it, but no bass player. We did two takes, and then I suggested that a twelve-string might give it a lot more fullness. I was almost sent on the errand to go to my shop and get a twelve-string when they decided it was too late and we scrapped it for the night."

"I remember 'You're a Big Girl Now' in particular," says Gregg Inhofer. "I feel like if I wanted to, I could say I contributed to the song. I couldn't play the organ part the way he wanted it because I wasn't very well versed in Hammond B-3 at the time. He wanted a certain kind of slide up the Hammond, and I tried it a few times before he said, 'No, man—here, you go play the piano, I'll play the organ.' And so I was learning the song on the piano and he was standing next to me when I played a third in the bass, an F sharp over the D chord, and he said, 'Hey, what's that? That's cool, I like that, keep that in.'"

Dylan overdubbed the song's flamenco guitar part and, with two numbers completed, deemed the evening's work done. The Minneapolis musicians left the studio reeling and euphoric and went back to their lives as brakemen and club musicians. For a few days, at least. Before Bob and David left, Paul Martinson hooked the Ampex machine up to a two-track Revox recorder and copied the rough mixes of the two songs down onto more manageable 7ips reels, which could be played on domestic reel-to-reel tape machines. Dylan took the recordings away with him to consider at his leisure.

EIGHT

DYLAN MUST HAVE LIKED WHAT HE HEARD, because before the weekend was over, the Zelenovich office called all the musicians to see if they could play further sessions. Bob, it seemed, was thrilled with the new versions of 'Idiot Wind' and 'You're a Big Girl Now,' and wanted to do a few more songs on the following Monday night, December 30. Were they available?

Were they ever! Apart from Gregg Inhofer, who was more of a fusion-jazz aficionado, the players were all big Dylan fans, who knew his back catalog backward, forward, and inside out and were able to gauge the value of that Friday's work.

"It was obvious to us at the time how good it was," says Kevin Odegard. "We knew we were part of the best new Dylan album in some time. As we drifted out of the first session, it was quite a feeling: We knew we had witnessed history. There's a guy in New York named Vinnie Fusco who is pictured in some of the Dylan biographies, a dark-haired man sitting in a chair behind the console during the recording of 'Like a Rolling Stone.' I met him later, when he was part of the production team for the record I did with David Zimmerman, and he said that during the '. . . Rolling Stone' session, he knew he was a witness to history being made. It's that same feeling that I'm referring to: It's obvious when you're there; it's an earth-shaking feeling—you know that nothing that you ever do will top this, and it's going to be something you can tell your grand-children about."

And quite apart from their place in history, there was the matter of hard cash to be considered. Even Inhofer, though less impressed than the others about playing with Dylan, was pleased to get the callback: "I said 'great,'" he admits, "'cause I'd gotten $300 on Friday. I was looking forward to getting another $300 on Monday."

On Saturday, Chris Weber was working at his music store when the woman from the Zelenovich office called to ask if he was available Monday for another session, and could he perhaps bring along a twelve-string guitar and a couple of harmonicas this time? Weber could do better than that: Ever the resourceful entrepreneur, he had become proactive and placed a couple of more musicians on standby, acting on an earlier remark of Dylan's.

"I had lined up a mandolin player and a banjo player, two of the best in the state—Peter Ostroushko on mandolin and Jim Tordoff on banjo—to be 'in the wings,' as it were," he explains, "because Bob had mentioned on Friday that he really wanted this to be an acoustic album, a return to his roots, if you will. So he was open to other traditional acoustic instruments, and I just let him know that I had two ace players if he wanted those instruments."

Weber selected a brand-new, top-of-the-line Guild 512 with a rosewood back and pearl inlay and took that along to the Monday session, together with the old Martin that Dylan had used the previous Friday. When Chris and his wife, Vanessa, arrived at the studio, they found Bob in the control room, deep in conversation with celebrated folk guitarist Leo Kottke about a song of Leo's called "So Cold in China," which Bob admired.

Clearly pleased with the results of the earlier session, Dylan seemed more relaxed this time, at ease with his accompanists, and open to suggestions. He produced a small red notebook in which were scribbled the verses to the first song he wanted to record that night. It was "Tangled Up in Blue," which would become one of his most popular songs and a staple of his concert sets for the next three decades. As before, Bob sat down and taught Weber the song, and after figuring out the capo position that he wanted to use on the twelve-string to create some higher sounds against the lower tones of Dylan's six-string guitar, Weber taught the other players the song. Dylan scrawled a few chords in the margin of a newspaper, tore it off, and handed this most skeletal of charts to Inhofer, saying, "Here's the chords to the next song." Then, while Paul Martinson and the musicians familiarized themselves with the song in readiness for a take, he tinkered with the lyric, refining it until the last moment. (Indeed, even long after the song had passed into the pantheon of rock classics, Dylan continued to play with it, changing a phrase here or a date there, altering characters' occupations and aspects, and generally exulting in the fluidity of the song's ever-shifting time scale and locations.)

At the New York sessions three months before, Dylan had recorded "Tangled Up in Blue" in the key of E, with an open-tuning configuration. In Minneapolis, he made a conscious decision to literally raise the pitch, kicking off the song in the key of G. But something was still missing from this arrangement. The song was just lying there tamely, not nearly as animated as the lyric demanded. After they played it through, he turned to Kevin Odegard, who sat next to him, tuning his guitar.

"How is it?" he asked. "What do you think?"

Before he could stop himself, Odegard found himself giving the kind of candid judgment that a star of Dylan's magnitude had probably not heard for the best part of a decade.

"It's . . . passable," he heard himself saying, almost before realizing what was happening. Here he was, telling the world's greatest living songwriter that his latest song was, in effect, pretty mediocre! What *was* he thinking of? He had let his guard down and thrown a curve ball at Bob Dylan, as relaxed as if he was among friends.

"*Passable?*" repeated Dylan, twisting his head slightly and giving Odegard that look he gives Donovan in *Don't Look Back,* that expression of mild incredulity that can shrivel an ego at fifty paces. Well, that's it, thought Odegard to himself, as his face turned beet red and the sweat coursed from his pores. I'm finished! I might as well go back to my

job on the railroad and tell my grandchildren about the day
that Dylan retired my number . . .

Frantically, Odegard sought to salvage the situation.

"Yeah, it's good," he added quickly, amending his opinion, "but I think it would be better, livelier, if we moved it
up to A with capos. It would kick ass up a notch."

Amazingly, his explanation seemed not only to placate
Dylan, but to intrigue him, too. Bob twisted his head,
looked around, then down at the floor, musing over the
guitarist's suggestion. Finally, he reached a decision, screw-
ing his shoe on the carpet as if extinguishing an invisible
cigarette.

"All right," he said, nodding. "Let's try it."

Weber and Odegard quickly moved their capos up two
frets to effect the key change. Dylan merely adjusted his fingered bar-chord positions, displaying the same skills in
transposition that had amazed Richard Crooks and Charlie
Brown in New York three months earlier. No capo for Bob,
thanks. They got halfway through the run-through before
Bob stopped, giving Paul Martinson his "Is it rolling, Bob?"
look. The key change had pushed the song up into the
higher reaches of Dylan's vocal range, and the enforced
change in his delivery brought a new intensity to the song,
which suddenly seemed more urgent and more intriguing;
the location jump-cuts between verses, flying past with real
cinematic slickness, whisking the listener from one scenario
to another with no uncomfortable grinding of verbal gears.
"It gave the song more urgency, and Bob started reaching
for the notes," Odegard later told *Rolling Stone* magazine.

"It was like watching Charlie Chaplin as a ballet dancer." Emboldened by the success of his first idea, Odegard added another, a lick he'd been noodling with since he'd heard something similar on a Joy of Cooking song called "Midnight Blues."

"It was a 'ring-a-ding-ding' figure that seemed to work well as an intro and a repeating figure on the front of each verse, so I stuck with it," explains Odegard. Weber's twelve-string adds body and romance to the arrangement, which is whipped along with peerless grace by the rhythm section: Bill Berg's delicate but sprightly snare and hi-hat work here is quite extraordinary, a true will-o'-the-wisp spirit at the heart of the song, and Billy Peterson has a ball embellishing the instrumental breaks with melodic bass figures that he would later regard as among his finest recorded work.

"I used a lot of suspensions, and I'm playing some melodic stuff that Paul Martinson brought up in the live take," says Peterson. "Even now, I look back and I don't know what I'd do differently now on that one; it's fine. The urgency of that suspension and release during the verses was more of a jazzy lyrical approach that Berg and I took. I stayed on the A when the band moved down to G, which was uncharacteristic of Dylan. You can hear us digging in. I got into that first take—I knew that was the one. Berg is popping on it."

Dylan was clearly excited by the revitalized song and delivered a stunning, mesmerizing performance on the first full take—moving and pitching at the microphone like a boxer evading his opponent's shots, dipping and rolling into his harmonica solo with the eloquent grace of a dragonfly. It was an unforgettable moment for the musicians. Like so many others in '60s stereoland, they were enraptured by the voice of a generation, and now here they were in a small room in South Minneapolis, surrounded by fellow dreamers, watching Dylan himself singing live into their headphones. And not singing just anything, but a song they all recognized was a classic, a future standard, something that would become a vital part of millions of lives. And they were right here at the eye of this cultural hurricane, a hurriedly thrown-together backing band, struggling to follow Dylan's dangerous, thrilling performance— and doing a pretty damn good job of it, too. They realized they would probably never record together again, and certainly not with Dylan; this was a once-in-a-lifetime ensemble that Paul Nelson of *Rolling Stone* magazine would later describe as "that wonderful pseudonymous band from Minnesota, who clearly have an affinity for Dylan and his music."

■ ■ ■

It wasn't just the musicians who had an affinity for Dylan and his music, though; a large part of the credit for the impact of these recordings must go to engineer Paul Martinson, whose fastidious choice and placement of microphones were matched by his instinctive grasp of the appropriate weight and balance of the various elements in the performances.

"I knew what my setup would be," Martinson explains. "I knew virtually all the players, I knew what microphones I wanted to use, and I had a lot of confidence in the room and the equipment we were using. Sound 80 was designed so the room would have very good sightlines between the players, and also between the control room and the players, so the engineer and producer could see everyone.

"We used a lot of Neumann U87 mikes, because at the time there was absolutely nothing better as a vocal mike. We also used them on pianos, guitars, electric guitar amps, zithers, bagpipes—everything! We almost always used the cardioid pattern with the 87s. Our guitar mikes were AKG 451s, which I tried to aim a little bit up the neck from the sound hole of the guitar; pointed straight at the sound hole, you get a lot of the low end and not enough harmonics. The kick drum mike was a Shure M57, and the drum set overheads were two Neumann KM 86s, small condenser mikes we also used for strings. The snare was another Shure M57—not the most expensive mike in the world, but one of the best. For the B-3 organ, we had a PM86 on the Leslie, and an SM5 on the regular speaker. The piano mikes were stereo, probably U87s or 451s."

The same attention to detail was applied to the foldback facilities, which allowed the musicians to hear themselves while playing.

"The headphones were 'open air' Sennheisers, for vocals. The advantage in using them was that you heard what's in the mix and what was live right next to you, at the same time. We used closed 'can'-type headphones for the bass player and drummer, who wanted all their information from the headphone mix. We worked very hard on our headphone systems—we dedicated two separate amps and several buses, providing a separate stereo amplifier for each mix."

In this respect, Martinson appears to have gone to great lengths to provide the Minneapolis musicians with a stronger cue than his mentor Phil Ramone had three months earlier in New York, and to Bob Dylan, it made all the difference in the world: Five Minneapolis takes would replace the hard work done earlier by Ramone and the hamstrung Weissberg band on the Columbia Records release.

Martinson continues his rundown of the sessions' technical specifications. "The recording board was a sixteen-track MCI 416-B with twenty-four inputs—what they called an 'over and under' console," he explains. "I didn't have to do a tremendous amount of experimenting with placement in the stereo image: The lead vocal was always going to be in the middle, and the kick drum and bass always went to the center—vinyl records would actually skip if the bigger sounds were not in the center.

"Bob's vocal was through a Neumann U87 with a 2db, 10k shelving and a delayed EMT echo. We ran a tape loop on a Revox deck—the same method as Phil Ramone used, except he used an Ampex deck—which was a really good way to get a short delay, of around 73 milliseconds. EMT set at 0.2 seconds. We used a Pandora Compressor on Dylan's vocal throughout. And we used some echo on the guitars and piano."

As on the Friday session, Martinson recorded a 15ips "safety" mix while the song was being played, using 3M Scotch tape, locally manufactured, on an Ampex 300 deck with Innovonics custom tape electronics. ("If you change the tape," he warns, "you have to recalibrate, re-bias and re-EQ the machine.")

"Except for 'Idiot Wind,' they were all very early takes," Martinson recalls. "'Lily, Rosemary and the Jack of Hearts' had never been played all the way through, and you can hear all the players reacting to the lyrics. Berg was just having fun—he varies his patterns throughout, and he was playful with it. The song is kind of like that, a big story song. Everybody knows it's a fantasy, but it's got all these interesting characters in it, so you're intrigued. You can hear me playing with the mix a little: The overall level and adjustments shift throughout the tune. I hit something near the end that I really liked, and I played it out till the end, always thinking I was gonna remix it—I was working on the relationship between the bass and the kick drum, in real time. The kick drum is very important in this record; this was in the days before disco, so it's pretty much natural. Berg made sure it sounded right in the room, and he'd tune it a little with the pegs to get it just right."

■ ■ ■

After they had nailed "Tangled Up in Blue," the musicians relaxed awhile before Dylan became restless and picked up the old Martin 0042G to start work on the next song, which was "Lily, Rosemary and the Jack of Hearts." Realizing that neither of the harmonicas he had brought along was in the same key as the song (D), Chris Weber asked his wife, Vanessa—eight-and-a-half months pregnant at the time—to dash back to the shop and find a harmonica in the appropriate key. In the meantime, Dylan worked closely with Berg and Peterson on the song's rhythmic structure, the latter stroking his acoustic double bass as Berg meticulously honed his drum patterns to Dylan's specifications.

Before they started recording, David Zimmerman came out of the control booth to warn Gregg, Billy, and Bill of the song's inordinate size, just as Bob himself had years before in Nashville when recording "Sad Eyed Lady of the Lowlands" with a local session crew more used to three-minute pop and country songs.

"This is a long song, just keep playing," David instructed the musicians. "When you think it ends, it doesn't, so just keep on playing."

Dylan rehearsed just long enough to get the groove where he wanted it, then, eager to catch the moment, spontaneously recorded "Lily, Rosemary and the Jack of Hearts," using one of the harmonicas Chris Weber had originally supplied. "It was a lot of fun, like going to the movies for everyone," says Odegard. "One complete take, and that song was in the can."

As with "Tangled Up in Blue," Berg and Peterson nailed the song immediately. "I played 'Lily, Rosemary and the Jack of Hearts' straight through on stand-up bass, one take, first time, no punches," says an understandably proud Billy

Peterson. "I had Bob's vocal cue turned down because I had to groove with Berg: I'd always have kick drum, snare, and hi-hat, my bass and Bob's guitar—Paul knew what I wanted to hear. I'd have plenty of time to listen to the rest later. That was a song that evolved, and you can hear the intensity, so I was keying off of some of the lyrics, but mainly staying in touch with Berg."

"'Lily, Rosemary and the Jack of Hearts' was a rollicking story song," recalls Weber. "The story was funny and the song was uptempo and easy to love, but the strangest thing about it is that Dylan played the wrong harmonica. Well, not the *wrong* harmonica necessarily, but it was certainly the wrong key for the song, which was in D. Dylan used an A harmonica on the song and can be heard throughout the introduction scrambling to find notes that worked on the mismatched instrument, which harmonized neither in the tonic position nor in a blues configuration, or 'cross-harp' styling. Bob struggled with the A harmonica and wandered around the melody looking for familiar chords, finding almost none. The really amazing thing is that the result almost acts as a perfect musical counterpoint to the story: A quizzical, puzzled feeling emerges from this take and went all the way to the pressing plant—but it works."

By the time that Vanessa Weber returned with a clutch of harmonicas in various keys—including the G harmonica wanted for "Lily, Rosemary and the Jack of Hearts," the song was done and dusted. Bob, though, was a perfect gentleman, solicitous about the impending addition to the Weber family. "He stood up and shook my hand when I came in," she recalls. "I sat down next to him and he asked when I was due, and he was really very friendly. He was just one of the guys."

David Zimmerman produced some of the album's record sleeves, assuring the musicians that, although it was impossible for their names to appear on this first batch of sleeves, they would eventually be accorded credit on later pressings.

"We were told that there were 100,000 jackets already printed with Eric Weissberg and Deliverance credited," remembers Chris Weber, "but if the album was a success and they printed more, they would give credit to the other musicians who were on the album."

At this point, Billy Peterson packed up his instruments and headed off for his nine o'clock gig, while the rest of the players finished off the session with "If You See Her, Say Hello," Bob adding some more of his flamenco guitar detailing, and Chris overdubbing twelve-string guitar in the later stages to give the tail end of the song a fuller sound. Dylan also wound up having to overdub a high-register mandolin part, when Peter Ostroushko proved unable to meet his requirements.

"Bob had asked Peter to play a fast flat-picking pattern up on the high end," recalls Weber, "and Peter, for whatever reasons, said, 'I don't know.' Bob just let it drop, then borrowed the instrument and did it himself." Nevertheless, Paul Martinson confirms, "Peter's mandolin part is still in there, back in the mix." (The next morning, Ostroushko called his pal Jim Tordoff to tell him all about the "strange dream"

he'd had the night before. Tordoff, who had driven Ostroushko from the 400 Bar to the session, cut him off mid-
sentence: "No, Peter, it really happened!")

With the basic tracks recorded, the musicians assembled
in the control room to hear playbacks, understandably excited by the quality of the performances.

"The most vivid thing for me was sitting in the control
room Monday night," recalls Weber, wistfully. "Dylan was
very pleased with 'Tangled Up in Blue.' The mood was very
'up' and we were all listening to the playback, and that was
really fun. Everybody was on the same plane, throwing comments out."

Each player was understandably attentive to his own
contribution. Kevin Odegard, for one, believed he had come
up with an appealing instrumental signature "hook" to the
start of each verse of "Tangled Up in Blue," urging Dylan to
retain it throughout: "Turn up that lead figure I was playing,
when you mix this—I really think you'll like it!" Dylan listened politely to his brother's protégé, only to ignore the appeal three days later at the mixdown session. Ultimately,
after the first couple of verses, it's the familiar jingle-jangle
tones of Chris Weber hammering out the third chord inver-
sion high up the neck of his Guild twelve-string that becomes the most prominent characteristic of the finished
version of "Tangled Up in Blue."

Though he was younger and less enamored of Dylan's
style of music than the others, the sessions nonetheless provided Gregg Inhofer with a swift education in studio technique and etiquette.

"The thing I learned the most from those sessions," he recalls, "was through watching Bill Berg, a jazz drummer whom I respected immensely. We're playin' 'Jack of Hearts,' and it's just a *dap-a-doo, dap-a-doo* riff, and I'm watching him listening to the playback with Bob, and I was so impressed with his concern that it was what Bob wanted. He said to Bob, 'Now, I can play it *dap-a-doo, dap-a-doo*, or *doop-a-dop-a-doop-a-dop-a-doop. . . .*' He was giving him all these options. I thought, this music must be, for all practical purposes, pretty low on the musical totem pole to him—but it wasn't. To see him show that much concern and give himself over as a tool, as an instrument—I was really impressed.

"That changed my whole attitude toward doing a session: From then on I always went in thinking, 'What does the producer or artist want from me?' It made me realize that my job is to give them what they want, because it's their vision, their music, not mine."

Inhofer wasn't the only one who admired the delicacy and aptness of Bill Berg's drumming. Indeed, Dylan himself was so impressed with the lift Berg gave to his songs that he took the drummer aside and asked if he'd be interested in joining Bob's road band for his upcoming European tour. Astonishingly, Berg turned down the opportunity, explaining that he had other plans: Although he was prepared to delay his cherished dream move to California for a few days of studio work with a living legend, any more extensive postponement, he felt, would constitute a betrayal of his longer-term ambitions. The others, who hadn't dared dream of such a development, were aghast at his refusal.

"The rest of us in the studio, thinking he was being re-cruited, were sitting there drooling," recalls Odegard, "with our tongues hanging out of our mouths, wondering, 'Is it our turn next? Is he going to ask the whole bunch of us to go?' But it was not to be.

"Bill Berg was a genius of percussion and has proven so also in his second career as an animator for Walt Disney. When he got to Venice, California, he found life as a session musician wasn't as wonderful as it was in Minneapolis, where he was the biggest fish in a small pond. So he pursued animation—I believe *The Great Mouse Detective* was his first film, and he was the lead, or 'hero,' animator for many of those Disney films. He still plays drums in Los Angeles, however, with the Wayne Johnson Band. He did the illustration of us in the studio—it's exactly the way I remember things, a remarkable feat of memory to carry it around for twenty-five years and be able to re-create it that well."

■ ■ ■

As before, Paul Martinson ran off a copy of the evening's songs for Dylan to consider, and David asked him to return two days later, on New Year's Day, to do a final mix with the brothers. The mixdown session proved easier, and shorter, than anyone expected.

"We started mixing 'Tangled Up in Blue,'" recalls Martinson. "As engineers do, I started cleaning things up, working the guitars, separating things out, and so on. We got so far, and Bob said, 'I really don't like this.' I said, 'Oh my gosh, what do you want to hear?' So he pulled out a copy I had made for him of the rough studio mix we had done the night of the session, and said, 'I want it to sound like *this!*'

"Because it was the only machine I had available at that time in the room, I had made the mix to our best two-track recorder at 15ips, so I thought that if there was nothing wrong level-wise, we might as well go ahead and release it that way. Then we proceeded to do that with all of them except 'Idiot Wind,' which I had surmised from the studio playback would be a little tough for the mastering engineer to put on a disk—it just needed a little more control of some levels, and so on. There's a lot of powerful instrumentation in that track, and a lot of dynamics, some high-flying peaks that needed to be brought under control. Bob said, 'Okay, go ahead and do that, but don't change the basic sound of it.' So we really didn't mix them, in the sense of doing more EQ or compression or any of that kind of stuff, the way you usually do."

In a remarkable testimony to Martinson's engineering and fly-mixing capabilities, that's how the Minneapolis tracks of *Blood on the Tracks* arrived at the pressing plant, with four of the five songs virtually untouched live two-track safety mixes. The studio in which they were recorded, however, no longer exists. Instead, according to Martinson, the same building now houses a company that tests products for acoustic properties—few of which, one imagines, could be as magical as the results of those two nights' sessions from three decades ago.

As they were about to leave, Billy Peterson turned up to collect his various instruments. Dylan was already ensconced in his car, but as Peterson walked across the parking lot, he wound down his window and hailed the bassist. "Man, I just want to tell you how great you played on this record, man, and what we have here," said Bob, evidently delighted with the results.

"I'll never forget that," says Peterson. "He must have been thinking, 'Whoa, my brother pulled this one off!' He *really* dug it. David never gets any credit for putting all that together: He hired these jazz heads to be the rhythm section and put the pieces of that band together so it would work for Bob.

"It's brilliant in the way it went down. It could have easily been a disaster, too. Who knew? David did."

NINE

WITH THE FIVE NEW RECORDINGS INSERTED into the track sequence, the two-track master tapes for the new version of *Blood on the Tracks* were hand-delivered to California by Mrs. Mark Zelenovich on a commercial airliner, in time to meet Columbia Records' January 4 pressing-plant deadline. As the record was being manufactured, packaged, and prepared for shipping, Monica Bay, a student writer at the University of Minnesota, scooped the worldwide entertainment media on Bob Dylan's hometown visit with a piece in the January 10 edition of the *Minnesota Daily*.

"Bob Dylan was in town over the holidays," she wrote, "and snuck quietly into Sound 80 studios to rework a few tracks on his upcoming Columbia LP, *Blood On The Tracks*. Apparently, he was not completely satisfied with all of the previously recorded songs, and enlisted the help of local musicians Bill Berg, Bill Peterson and Kevin Odegard for the retakes. None of the song titles have been changed."

The news that Dylan had rerecorded some of the songs came as a considerable surprise to the original New York session team—not least to Phil Ramone, who despite being the album's de facto producer, had been left completely in the dark about the singer's misgivings.

"Oh yeah, I was quite shocked," says Ramone, adding with a chuckle, "I thought he was quite happy with what he had! But like I say, it doesn't take much, when you're sitting around with the tape for three or four months, playing it for friends, and somebody says, 'Wouldn't it be great if there were horns there, or some great electric guitar or pedal steel, or something?' to change your mind. Generally, you try those ideas out when you're on the road, and either you improve on your album or you don't. "I had no say in what that was gonna be at the moment that he changed it—that's why I think if the originals come out and the bootlegs get thrown aside, it would be a nice gift to the public. I think if you're interested in Bob Dylan, that's got to be a landmark, in that it's the original, as is."

As he was caught up in a blizzard of session dates and Deliverance concerts, it was some time before Eric Weissberg heard that some of the tracks had been redone. He took the news philosophically.

"I felt perhaps it was because we were not given enough time or direction to make what we did what he wanted," Weissberg believes. "Since we were all very experienced accompanists and very good players, to say the least, we felt we could have done what he wanted, given a fair shake. And I would say that we were all somewhat bummed about it. But I feel absolutely no bitterness about it. This happens from time to time."

Charlie Brown was rather less sanguine about the situation. "I was pissed, frankly!" he admits. "The first thing that hit me was 'How dare you? You've got some of the best damn players on the planet playing on your record, and you *replaced* it?' Then I just thought, 'That's kind of the way he is.' Eric said the same thing—'That's just the way Bob is.' I have two copies of the album, but I'm a little reluctant to play it—I'm afraid it might piss me off!"

Tom McFaul was the least bothered about being replaced. "When I heard that, it did not surprise me at all," he admits. "I didn't feel I contributed anything useful."

Richard Crooks, meanwhile, was too busy to give much of a damn about it, one way or the other. "By then I was on to other sessions, and it didn't bother me," he claims. "It was his record; he has every right to do whatever he wants with it. But I would have liked to have my name on the record because everybody says, 'Oh, I thought you said you played on this?' and I have to explain I was part of the group Deliverance. I don't even know if we made it onto the second printings or not."

Crooks might consider himself fortunate to get even that meager acknowledgment, compared to the Minneapolis musicians, who have remained anonymous and uncredited since the album was released, a snub that, as we will see in the next chapter, still rankles three decades later. But as they were assured of due credit on subsequent pressings, there was nothing to sour their excitement when, on Monday, January 20, 1975, Columbia Records released *Blood on the Tracks* with a series of simultaneous "listening parties" for media, retailers, and record company promotional troops in major cities across the United States.

In New York, the party at Columbia's A&R Studio A reportedly included a visit from Dylan, paying respects to his mentor, John Hammond. In Minneapolis, the Sound 80 party kicked off with food, drinks, and the jaw-dropping, radio-friendly opener "Tangled Up in Blue." Promotional giveaways at these events included melted-down black vinyl paperweights with the album's distinctive red Columbia label pasted on both sides, along with official *Blood on the Tracks* railroad engineer's caps, hanging paper mobiles, and rack cards for retailers. Similar events were held in Chicago, Los Angeles, San Francisco, Nashville, Miami, and, a few days later, London.

Artemis Records chairman and CEO Danny Goldberg remembers well the day he got his promotional copy of *Blood on the Tracks*. "I was working for Led Zeppelin's label Swan Song when I got an advance cassette of *Blood on the Tracks* from a friend at Columbia," he recalls. "The next day I flew to Chicago, where Zeppelin was on tour, and where they were being interviewed for a *Rolling Stone* cover story by Cameron Crowe. I remember bringing the treasure of the new Dylan album into Robert Plant's suite at the Ambassador Hotel and listening to it with Robert and Cameron. Here we were: Robert, who was one of the world's biggest rock stars; Cameron, writing for the world's most important rock magazine; and me, doing my best to pretend to be a savvy PR guy—and we were all as overwhelmed, impressed, and delighted by *Blood on the Tracks* as if we were in ninth grade.

"Blood on the Tracks is one of Dylan's greatest albums," Goldberg continues. "It is also the first of Dylan's 'adult' albums, in which he is starting to look back on his younger days in songs like 'Tangled Up in Blue' and 'If You See Her, Say Hello.' For a baby boomer like me, who was a teenager when *Blonde on Blonde* and *Highway 61* came out, the lyrics on *Blood on the Tracks* were the first inkling that the rock art form that said so much about the inner life of someone in high school could also speak to the passions of our generation as we got older."

■ ■ ■

The final version of *Blood on the Tracks* featured just ten songs, perfectly sequenced to present a subtly undulating succession of moods and mannerisms.

The new version of "Tangled Up in Blue" kicks the proceedings off in sprightly style, rolling in on the back of Bill Berg's feather-light hi-hat tattoo. The change of key instigated at the Minneapolis session brings a freshness and immediacy to Dylan's delivery of the opening lines that's perfectly in keeping with the first verse's early-morning setting. From there, the band pushes things along with gusto, Chris Weber's ringing twelve-string lending a buoyant charm to Dylan's tale.

An exercise in reminiscence, "Tangled Up in Blue" is perhaps the most immediately satisfying demonstration of how art teacher Norman Raeben's insights had affected Dylan's writing. Opening with the protagonist ruminating from his morning bed about his past, it moves swiftly from scene to scene, in a series of daring jump cuts sketching archetypal scenes from American bohemian life. With the aspect constantly shifting between third person and first person (indeed, such distinctions seem endlessly fluid: Even between the New York and Minneapolis sessions, the protagonist's first appearance had switched from "he" to "I"), this isn't just Dylan's journey; it's the one undertaken, in one form or another, by an entire generation.

The first verse finds our subject musing briefly on his youthful sweetheart, before outlining how their young love was foiled by parental disapproval, leaving him outside in the rain (a recurrent motif on *Blood on the Tracks*, indicative of romantic failure and heartbreak), hitchhiking to the East Coast to "pay [his] dues"—just as the teenage Robert Zimmerman had made his way to Greenwich Village in New York to establish his folksinging credentials.

The second verse finds him involved in a liaison with a married woman (as was Sara when Bob first met her), which ends in failure. "We drove that car as far as we could/ Abandoned it out West," sings Dylan, employing an automotive metaphor that could easily be read as analogizing the Dylans' move to California, which many view as the decisive factor in the collapse of their marriage. Alone again, our itinerant hero drifts in the space of a few lines from the "Great North Woods" to New Orleans—riding Highway 61, one presumes—in the third verse. "But all the while I was alone/The past was close behind," he admits, betraying the need—which artists share with drifters—to escape being defined by his own past.

It's impossible to tell whether the girl he finds working in a topless bar in the fourth verse is the same one that initially triggered his reminiscence—and ultimately, it's as irrelevant as the oft-posed speculation about whether she's intended to be an oblique reference to Sara, who, of course, worked as a Playboy bunny before she met Bob. The figure's importance lies more in the aesthetic epiphany she induces in the protagonist by having him read "an Italian poet from the 13th century"—most likely Dante Alighieri, whose trilogy *The Divine Comedy* describes the structure of the cosmos and the workings of love (both divine and human), with a psychological acuity that chimes percipiently with the attitudes and beliefs of our own era.

It's one of several references on *Blood on the Tracks* to the notion of aesthetic redemption, leading smoothly into the bohemian wonderland of the sixth verse, where Montague Street in Brooklyn is a hotbed of intellectual activity with "music in the cafes at night, and revolution in the air." But then darkness intrudes into paradise—the references to "dealing with slaves" and how the girl "froze up inside" are surely metaphors for hard drugs—and our man ends up on the move again.

Finally, he resolves, in the last verse, to return to his youthful sweetheart, who presumably represents the last stable moment he can recall in a life that long ago broke free from its moorings. But even as he decides to look her up, he realizes that she, like "all the people we used to know," will probably be "an illusion to me now." The song ends with him once again resigned to his rootless fate, "still on the road, heading for another joint," striding cheerfully off into his future, a jolly troubadour blowing breezily on his harmonica.

The performance is so utterly engaging that the song's seven verses fly by in the twinkling of an eye. At no point is the listener, like the protagonist, allowed to rest or become mired in one location before being whisked off again. One's gaze is allowed to fall for just the briefest moment, expected to really *see* what's happening at a glance, the way Norman Raeben expected his pupils to *see* what they were painting in an instant. And with every glimpse, each successive detail plucked from memory—past, present, and future—loses its grip on our perception. Time is everything yet nothing in "Tangled Up in Blue": Unlike in more straightforward linear narratives, time recedes, rather than grows, in importance as the song progresses. Although the song is in one important sense *about* time—about the way it pulls us apart, propels us in new directions, and colors our recollections—the song occupies a timeless space, a kind of "everytime" for everyman to live through.

The effect is something like an out-of-body experience, with the listener, led by the protagonist, effectively floating above events as they transpire, glancing this way and that from scene to scene, back and forth in time, observing from several different aspects as the situation—which is, of course, the hero's emotional development—unfolds. It's an aesthetic experience akin to the fanciful, evocative paintings of Marc Chagall, particularly the famous depiction of two lovers floating across the sky above a little town: There's exactly the same sense of detachment *from* reality leading to a deeper insight *into* that reality.

"I was never really happy with it," claimed Dylan of "Tangled Up in Blue" in the sleeve notes to *The Bootleg Series, Volumes 1–3*. "I guess I was just trying to make it like a painting where you can see the different parts but then you also see the whole of it. With that particular song, that's what I was trying to do . . . with the concept of time, and the way the characters change from the first person to the third person, and you're never quite sure if the third person is talking or the first person is talking. But as you look at the whole thing it really doesn't matter."

The way that the exhilaration of "Tangled Up in Blue" gives way to the wistful reflection of "Simple Twist of Fate" is only the first of several masterstrokes of track sequencing on *Blood on the Tracks*. The mood is strikingly different, its crepuscular tone—reminiscent of Thomas Gray's poem "Elegy in a Country Churchyard"—economically established by the opening lines, in which the star-crossed lovers first meet.

The song is a brief encounter between strangers who meet, have one night together, and then part. They share apparent intimacy, but their attitudes are poles apart, it's clear: To her it means nothing; to him it's everything. Departing before he wakes the next morning, she forgets him almost before she's out the door, but his life is cursed forever by her memory. Dylan's voice is sad, reflective, but with a tart tang of pain burning the edges of his apparent equanimity, scorching through completely in the series of "ate" rhymes (*straight, freight, gate, wait,* and *late*), which serve as the thread linking the six verses together.

The scenes are etched in a few minimal details, some atmospheric (the old canal, the evening sky), some noir clichés (the neon light, and light breaking through a shade), some soundtrack cues (the distant saxophone), and some quirkier, Coen Brothers sorts of moments, like the ticking clocks and the parrot that talks. Often criticized by Dylan commentators, these latter images do, however, convey something of the desultoriness and solipsism of the loser, the sheer bereftness of his existence.

Dylan's delivery, though, is not so much bereft as detached, a numb recitation of memories that crumples into searing pain with the fourth line of each verse. The transition is particularly elegant in the fourth verse, where the line "Felt an emptiness inside to which he just could not relate" plummets—or soars, depending on your viewpoint—from quizzical detachment to abject desolation within the space of a heartbeat. It remains one of the most impressive vocal stratagems of Dylan's entire career.

Although the song can be read simply as an account of a doomed one-night stand, on another level it suggests why, perhaps, the couple were unable to connect more deeply. As so often on *Blood on the Tracks*, it's down to the conflict between art and life within an artist's life, the way that the artist's detached, observational imperative inevitably impairs his or her ability to foster relationships. Throughout their liaison here, the narrator's attention is not on the woman so much as on his surroundings—the details listed above. We learn plenty about the location, the atmosphere, the sights and sounds, but we learn nothing at all of her, save that she can drop the entire event—and him—from her mind as easily as she drops a coin into a blind man's cup.

The fact that he can't relate to the "emptiness inside" suggests how ill equipped he is to deal with matters of the heart: The emptiness is not so much because she's gone as because he's realized his introverted detachment has condemned him to isolation. As he acknowledges in the final verse, "People tell me it's a sin/To know and feel too much within": Emotions are meant to be expressed, and so long as his feelings are kept within, there's little hope of connecting meaningfully with a prospective partner. In the case in question, why on earth would any woman want to hang around with someone who noticed everything but her, who could recall the shape and color and smell and sound of their every moment together but can't summon up even one detail about her?

Regarded on this level, "Simple Twist of Fate" is not just about the conflicting *needs* of an artist's craft (things like observation, rumination, and reflection) and those of his or her personal life, but also about the *embodiment* of that conflict, a demonstration of the very shortcomings that sabotage the artist's chances of emotional fulfillment. It's also, lest we lose sight of the fact, an exquisitely beautiful song: Score one for the artist, then.

Score two, in fact: "You're a Big Girl Now," which follows, is just as beautiful, one of the most heartbreaking love
plaints ever written, a masterpiece of emotional subtlety
tracking the increments of regret and desolation afflicting an
abandoned heart as it becomes more desperately aware of its
solitude.

The abruptness of the first two lines embodies the initial
shock of rejection, hinting at an earlier confident assurance
suddenly struck dead in its tracks. Then, *slam!* he's out in
the rain again, drenched in self-pity and wondering what
hit him. In each verse, the narrator tries to fool himself into
believing things aren't really that bad, with a series of
bland, hopeful images, but each time, the metaphor short-
circuits his thoughts back to the woman he's lost, as he desperately seeks redemption: "I'm out here in the rain—but
she's on dry land; that birdsong—it's like me singing to
you; time changes things—maybe I can change, too?" It's
futile, of course, and in each verse the rose-tinted equanimity of the first couple of lines is ultimately shattered by the
wracked moan that concludes line three, a razor across his
hopeful complacency that remains one of Dylan's most affecting vocal gambits. (The New York version is, if anything, even more emotionally naked than the rerecorded
version.)

With each verse, he becomes increasingly frantic as he realizes the futility of his quest, blurting out an impassioned "I
can change, I swear" exactly halfway through the song,
ratcheting the pain up a notch and laying the emotional
groundwork for the utter desolation that comes with the last

verse's bereft "I'm going out of my mind" and the final spike of that corkscrew to his heart, a blow that leaves him writhing in eternal torment.

The fragile interplay of drums and understated guitar provides a discreet setting for another painful lyric, as if delicately tiptoeing around sensitive emotional territory. The lovely Spanish guitar flourishes that accent the lines, meanwhile, lend a tearful dignity and courtliness to the account. The halting harmonica coda on which the song drifts out leaves the situation still unresolved, a lingering thread of pain that explains, but doesn't mitigate, the bumptious, spiteful tone of the ensuing "Idiot Wind," another brilliant coup of track sequencing.

"'You're a Big Girl Now,' well, I read that this was supposed to be about my wife," groused Dylan sarcastically in the *Biograph* sleeve notes. "I wish somebody would ask me first before they go ahead and print stuff like that. I mean it couldn't be about anybody else but my wife, right? Stupid and misleading jerks sometimes these interpreters are. . . . They never stop to think that somebody has been exposed to experiences that they haven't been . . . anyway it's not even the experience that counts, it's the attitude toward the experience. . . . I don't write confessional songs. Emotion's got nothing to do with it. It only seems so, like it seems that Laurence Olivier is Hamlet."

But if "You're a Big Girl Now" *seemed,* to some, to refer specifically to his split with Sara, it was harder still to try to read "Idiot Wind" as anything other than an outburst of cathartic rage triggered by their separation. And if it's not the experience that counts, so much as the attitude toward the experience, well, if ever a song had attitude, this is it. It's an extraordinary piece, as big a shock coming after the first three engagingly folksy, acoustic songs as Dylan's bile-fueled "electric" period was after his previous folk-protest period. Suddenly, the listener is plunged once again into the maelstrom of paranoia, blame, and reproach that characterized earlier songs such as "Like a Rolling Stone" and "Positively 4th Street." The song's sheer length—a shade under eight minutes—and burring organ reinforce that impression: This is a blistering, thorough diatribe, an outpouring of anger apparently prompted by a specific betrayal, but sprayed indiscriminately at whoever passes across the singer's radar. The exquisitely subtle jazz drumming from Bill Berg helps keep it from flagging, sustaining the tension level like someone walking across hot coals—the sonic equivalent of undergoing the kind of dressing-down that Dylan doles out here, lashing wildly about him, and occasionally hitting himself in the process.

Structured in four blocks, each containing two five-line verses followed by a five-line chorus, "Idiot Wind" is a vindictive condemnation of a couple too stupid and pigheaded to realize that they ought to persevere and try to work things out together, rather than stubbornly turn away from each other. Within it, we can glimpse veiled references to Dylan's own character—though, once again, not much is revealed of the song's leading woman—and come to some understanding of what he perhaps considers extenuating circumstances for earlier errant behavior. The sneering reiteration of "id-

iot" in the chorus—pronounced "eee-diott"—is surely derived from art teacher Norman Raeben's invocation to see
things as they really are. (According to Dylanologist Bert
Cartwright, who received confirmation from Raeben's
widow, the artist felt there was "an idiot wind blowing and
blinding all human existence.")

The first verse establishes the paranoid personality of a
rogue celebrity, a chic outlaw type, more notorious than famous—someone a bit like Dylan, in fact. The second verse
builds on this, moving from general annoyance at widespread misunderstanding of his art and his motives to a
more specific incredulity at his own partner's similarly poor
understanding of him. "Look," he's saying, "don't you have
any idea of what it's like to be me, to have to live as a legend, as misused, misunderstood public property? After all
these years together, you still have no comprehension of the
pressures that brings with it?" Pressures that, perhaps, demand their own compensatory indulgences—as hinted at
later when he admits, "You tamed the lion in my cage but it
just wasn't enough to change my heart."

The third verse features a succession of romantically
melodramatic images—a burning train wagon, lightning,
necromancy, crucifixion, and wars (plural)—which serve as
a fanciful setup for the pathos of the "I Will Survive" sentiment into which it resolves. The fourth verse opens with the
protagonist yet again dumped by the roadside (at least it's
not raining this time, if that's any consolation), then feints
with the reference to "visions of your chestnut mare" that
instinctively brings to mind Dylan's old friend and quondam

writing partner Roger McGuinn, who years before wrote and sang "Chestnut Mare" with The Byrds. It's entirely possible that Dylan felt betrayed by something McGuinn had said—maybe he's the one who'd been "planting stories in the press"?—but it's just as likely to be a diversionary tactic to distract attention from his own agenda.

The verse builds to a climax with Dylan relishing his detractors' eventual doom in lines—"One day you'll be in the ditch, flies buzzin' around your eyes, blood on your saddle"—that bring to mind Baudelaire's poem "The Carcass," from *Les Fleurs du Mal*, in which two lovers come across a rotting animal corpse: "The flies buzzed and hissed on these filthy guts . . . And you in your turn will be rotten as this." Dylan, of course, had long been a fan of the French symbolist poets, most recently mentioning Baudelaire in the sleeve notes to *Planet Waves* ("Duluth— where Baudelaire Lived & Goya cashed in his Chips"), shortly before he wrote the songs that made up *Blood on the Tracks*.

In the fifth verse, a Ferris wheel metaphor both extends the circus imagery of "lion in my cage" and allows the narrator to make a neat little point about moral relativism: "You'll find out when you reach the top, you're on the bottom." The sixth verse shifts from circus to ceremony, with images of institutionalized decay, both in the world about them, and in her face, now unrecognizable. In the chorus that follows, the reference to "Mardi Gras" that was in the New York version has been changed to the more declarative

"Grand Coulee Dam," which not only allows a hidden geographical pun (the wind now blows from Washington state to Washington, D.C.) but also reminds us that the song of that title was one of the three songs performed by Dylan and The Band at the Woody Guthrie Memorial Concerts in 1968, Dylan's first public appearances since his motorbike accident two years earlier.

The tide of disaffection reaches its fullest flow in the seventh verse, a howl of contempt for anything that reminds the narrator of his former lover—including the books she's read, an understandable aversion, because they would, of course, provide the most vivid expression of her personality and character. Repelled, he's off "down the highway" again, mention of which recalls the song of that title from Dylan's first album, one of his earliest recorded expressions of his essentially itinerant nature, to which he has no option but to return, "down the road to ecstasy"—a deliberate echo of William Blake's aphorism about how "the road of excess leads to the palace of wisdom," suggestive of his more indulgent, experiential nature.

By the eighth verse, he appears to have reached some acceptance of the two protagonists' differing characters and their conflicting tropes—toward creative pain, indulgence, and wanderlust on his part, and toward nurturing holiness on hers, representative on a wider scale of the classic opposition of masculine and feminine traits. The song closes with the scornful chorus now directed at both parties: "We're idiots, babe, it's a wonder we can even feed ourselves." It's a mockingly exultant conclusion to an exuberant, impassioned performance that, in its official version, leaves both singer and listener emotionally drained. The discarded New York recordings are by contrast slower, wearier, and more resigned in tone, entirely lacking in the anger of the Minneapolis version, but in one case compensated for by the ghostly breaths of organ that float up through the chorus like a pang of sadness bringing a lump to the throat.

In yet another dazzlingly effective coup de sequence, the fury of "Idiot Wind" is followed by the balm of "You're Gonna Make Me Lonesome When You Go," a fond farewell to a departed lover. Various lyric references point to its being directed at Ellen Bernstein, the Columbia A&R operative with whom Dylan had a liaison through the summer of 1974: Besides mentions of her birthplace, Ashtabula, and her homes in San Francisco and Honolulu, there is a reference to Queen Anne's lace, a plant that she pointed out to him while they were walking in the fields around Dylan's Minnesota farm. If so, it's the most touching parting gift one could wish for.

The tone is light and affectionate but noncommittal, an expression of the easy nature of their relationship, its lack of baggage or expectations. It's matched by the musical setting, which is the easiest, least mannered treatment on the album. There's no room here for regret or reproach; instead, the bridge following the third verse conjures up only happy, positive memories of a bucolic paradise that surely echoes life on The Farm, with a slow-running river, crickets serenading each other, and flowers "bloomin' crazy," a wonderful evocation of summer fecundity.

The song features yet another mention of poets—this time comparing his previous relationships to "Verlaine's and Rimbaud." This is presumably a reference to the turbulent nature of the French symbolists' mutual fascination, in which the teenager Arthur Rimbaud's extreme antisocial behavior exposed the more superficial nature of his older mentor Paul Verlaine's bohemian attitudes. After such fiery relationships, one infers, it's a pleasure to be involved in one with no equivalent emotional baggage, one where he can simply be himself, without worrying about his behavior.

"Meet Me in the Morning," which opens the second side, is the most basic, generic distillation of pain on the whole album. It's a classic twelve-bar blues structure of six verses, each with a repeated first line and subsequent resolution, with the particulars boiled away to a bare residue of traditional blues imagery: roosters crowing, darkness before dawn, hound dogs, barbed wire, and even a hailstorm, the latest bout of inclement weather to afflict our hapless protagonist on *Blood on the Tracks*. Musically, it's the most successful of the New York band's recordings, with some lovely, lazy interplay of steel-string acoustic guitar picking, electric guitar detailing, and Buddy Cage's slow-burning thread of pedal steel guitar lurking, ready to pounce once the sixth verse is over.

At nearly nine minutes, "Lily, Rosemary and the Jack of Hearts" is the longest track on the album, and the least emotionally involving. Hustled along by brisk strumming and sprightly snare and bedded in a churchy organ pad, it's a Wild West movie, sketched with verve and ambiguity, in broad mythic strokes akin to old folk ballads, but delivered like saloon-bar gossip. There's a shifty, furtive quality to the piece, and Dylan's vocal is loaded with incredulity, further confusing matters.

The story is a blur of action, its interior voice and aspect constantly switching from character to character and location to location, proceeding at such speed that it's virtually impossible to latch on to its narrative thrust until it's all over—and then you're still not quite sure what you've just "witnessed." So, Big Jim's been stabbed by his wife, Rosemary, who's heading for the gallows—but she's suicidal anyway, so that's okay—and the Jack of Hearts has skipped with the bank loot, leaving Lily washing her hair. That's it? Or is it a parable of gender stereotyping, in which rogue outlaw males usurp their elders, while their concubines follow a parallel cycle, flourishing, blooming briefly, then dying—a wheel of codependency cycling endlessly around, forever doomed to failure?

Although the longest, it's the weakest song on the album, more dependent than the other tracks on the mood of its performance—as demonstrated by the discarded New York version, which simply lies there, flat and lifeless. The Minneapolis musicians, by contrast, manage to animate it more by attacking it with hearty gusto. But although it's an accomplished piece of plotting on Dylan's part, there's little of the resonance that accompanies previous Dylan narratives of comparable length.

"If You See Her, Say Hello" is a wistful paean to an old flame, a more mature, affecting equivalent to "Girl of the North Country," although with her probable location now shifted from Dylan's north country homeland to Tangier in Morocco, the North African base for expatriate American bohemians like William S. Burroughs and Paul Bowles. Clearly, this is a different type of woman from the wholesome blond farmgirl of the earlier song, a more exotic bloom entirely. The singer is accordingly less solicitous about her well-being; he knows she's worldly enough to take care of herself, and he seems more concerned about letting her know how he is, how he respects her bid for freedom, and how she's welcome to look him up anytime. Where the subject of "Girl of the North Country" is firmly and irrevocably in the past, a memory rather than a need, he's still carrying a torch for this one—as he acknowledges, "She still lives inside of me, we've never been apart."

It's the most poignant vocal performance of the album, a tender reminiscence not quite toughened into Bogart-like resilience: "And I've never gotten used to it, I've just learned to turn it off/Either I'm too sensitive, or else I'm getting' soft." Well, obviously, he's too sensitive by half—he has no choice—although the idiom tells of a certain philosophical resignation. That's revealed as a sort of inverse bravado, however, in the final verse, which finds him, ever the observant recorder, replaying the past scene by scene, sensation by sensation, trying to keep alive the particular intensity of feeling associated with her memory.

With moody organ tinting and minimal percussive detailing behind the web of gentle guitar arpeggios and mandolin counterpoint, "If You See Her, Say Hello" is the ultimate demonstration here of engineer Paul Martinson's skill at recording and mixing acoustic stringed instruments—particularly on the exquisite, aching coda of doubled-up mandolins and twelve-string guitars that concludes the song.

Another brilliant shift of gears dispels the lump in the throat left by "If You See Her, Say Hello" with the more melodramatic flourishes of "Shelter from the Storm," shifting vertiginously from personal intimacy to mythic allegory. Gone is the bruised and tender narrator of the preceding song, replaced by a haunted figure plucked from chaos and impending doom by a salvatory, Madonna-like figure.

It's hard not to read "Shelter from the Storm," even more than "You're a Big Girl Now" and "Idiot Wind," in terms of Bob and Sara. The first verse alone, with its references to "another lifetime" of "toil and blood," inverted virtues, and a road of mud, surely represents his bachelor life, conveying the exhausting treadmill of Dylan's 1966 world tour in the heightened, macrocosmic manner of Greek epic poems such as Homer's *Iliad* and *Odyssey*.

It's essentially another account of the interrelatedness and mutual need felt between the wild-spirited male and the nurturing female, the classic Taoist principles of yin and yang that help sustain the balance of the world. The first five verses are effusive and grateful, the narrator repeatedly explaining the travails of a "world of steel-eyed death" from which she has rescued him—a catalog of poison, exhaustion, abuse, and, of course, another hailstorm—before suddenly walking slap-bang into "a wall between us" in the sixth verse, the result of some unspecified lack of respect on his own part. Once again, although he offers plenty of information, both factual and allegorical, about his own circumstances, we learn precious little about her—the only description he provides depicts her as an idealized, fairytale figure, "with silver bracelets on her wrists and flowers in her hair."

From there, it's downhill all the way, a brief catalog of the desolation that ensues when yin slips out of balance with yang—crying babies; mourning doves; an oppressive Wild West trinity of deputy, preacher, and undertaker; and general hopelessness and doom—with the bereft protagonist eventually stranded in the back of beyond, left naked and forlorn as Jesus, his clothes gambled over by latter-day centurions. Without the support system she provided, he's quite unable to cope, just a junkie for her love: "I bargained for salvation an' they gave me a lethal dose."

The song features another masterful performance from Dylan, his haunted vocal—especially in the opening verses—chiming perfectly with the mythic imagery of torment. The setting, meanwhile, is simple and direct, its stripped-down manner likewise befitting the way in which the protagonist is stripped of his dignity. It was reportedly recorded by just Dylan and Tony Brown—but isn't that a second guitar adding a low-register counterpoint to Dylan's strummed acoustic? Either that or Tony Brown is doing some neat bass chording on this track.

In the context of the catalog of pain and regret that makes up the bulk of *Blood on the Tracks,* the decision to end the album with "Buckets of Rain," rather than the more convoluted "Up to Me," is obviously correct. Though interesting in itself, "Up to Me" only confuses matters, leaving the narrator's attitude toward what are clearly life-shattering events far too coded and unresolved.

By contrast, "Buckets of Rain" brings a sense of closure to the matter—or if not complete closure, then at least an air of equanimity. Dylan's lovely, spiky guitar picking lends an honest, positive air to the song, like fresh air following a thunderstorm; the simplicity of the setting likewise implies a New Start, a moving on with one's life, taking consolation, when it comes, with gratitude, and bearing misfortune with courage and dignity. The melody echoes that of Tom Paxton's "Bottle of Wine," as does the song's blithe, consolatory manner: This isn't weary resignation, desolation, or reproach, as in the preceding songs; it's a more resilient attitude, shot through with hope and endurance.

There's a deceptive, nursery-rhyme-like simplicity, almost a kind of gaiety, to the song that's entirely refreshing, echoing the tenor of old folk and country-blues songs. It's there from the start, in the sheer inebriated silliness of the first verse, slipping easily between daffy, playfully romantic images—buckets coming out of ears, buckets of moonbeams—like a tipsy busker after a skinful. There's still time, in the third verse, for a beautifully understated moment of regret, when four lines of effusive praise and devotion are finessed with the payoff line "Everything about you is bringing me misery," revealing at least one little corner of the singer's heart that remains in shadow, for all his optimism.

Counterbalancing it is the previous verse's "Friends will arrive, friends will disappear," which finds him finally acknowledging the shifting, cyclical nature of relationships, learning to accept that the orbits of different lives intersect all too briefly, then head off again, following their own disparate arcs. Finally, the album closes on the philosophical observation that "Life is sad, life is a bust/All you can do is do what you must," a resolution that draws the sting of the preceding torments, freeing the protagonist from his torrid past into the flux of an eternal present.

■ ■ ■

Columbia was happy to have Dylan back in the fold with a three-record deal that would include the long-bootlegged *Basement Tapes* and *Desire*, the latter becoming a huge bestseller on the back of *Blood on the Tracks*, which flew out of the stores immediately upon its release, achieving tremendous word-of-mouth recognition before the powerful lobby of rock critics could pass judgment. It became Dylan's second chart-topping studio album in little over a year, following *Planet Waves*. *Blood on the Tracks* sold swiftly, gaining a Gold Disc (for half a million sales) on February 12, a mere three weeks after its release, making it the fastest and bestselling Dylan album ever until that time.

New York, Dylan's "other" hometown, wasted no time in publishing two quick reviews in successive issues of the *Village Voice*. In the January 27 edition, Robert Christgau referred to "a certain anonymous brightness" imposed on the proceedings by the "unknown Minneapolis studio musicians" but admitted that the most striking thing about the album was the music's sheer beauty. "By second hearing its loveliness is almost literally haunting, an aural déjà vu," he wrote. "There are moments of anger that seem callow, and the prevailing theme of interrupted love recalls adolescent woes, but on the whole this is the man's most mature and assured record." He gave it an A rating.

Paul Cowan's review, which followed in the February 3 edition, was more circumspect. Focusing on the obvious inferences of marital disharmony underlying the songs, he portrayed the album as "the excruciating cry of a man who is tormented by his own freedom," a cri de coeur from a man trapped by his art. "Dylan bears a very special kind of curse," Cowan believed. "He seems unable to establish warm, lasting relationships, but he's too eager for love to make the cold decision to sacrifice his private life to his art, as Joyce or even Mailer can. *Blood* . . . is a great album because he's writing into the headwinds of that curse . . ."

Robert Shelton, who had been Dylan's earliest media champion, took issue with Cowan's review. "Cowan's psycho-critique misunderstood Dylan's role playing," he felt. "Would he say Shakespeare was guilt-ridden because Lady Macbeth washed her hands, or that the bard was indecisive because Hamlet was conflicted? Even if *Blood On the Tracks* was literally confessional, Cowan is a less-than-humane witness to a catalog of remorse, self-doubt and chagrin . . . Dylan has wanted to be liked, but he tried to balance that need with trying to be true to his many embattled artistic selves."

Time magazine, reviewing *Blood on the Tracks* alongside albums from such giants as Henry Gross, Arthur Hurley & Gottlieb, and Neil Sedaka, was sniffily dismissive of Dylan's latest work, considering "You're a Big Girl Now" just a lesser "Just Like a Woman," and claiming its chief characteristic was "inconsistency," before grudgingly concluding that "overall, longtime fans will approve of Dylan's return to an older, sparser folk style."

Rolling Stone magazine, perhaps stung by one too many Dylan "comeback" projects in recent years, tiptoed into the *Blood on the Tracks* arena with a tentative report in the "Random Notes" column of their February 13 edition outlining the basic circumstances behind the album's creation, and according all the Minneapolis musicians their first national public credit. "A first run of album covers has already been printed, so the north country boys won't get a credit until the second pressing," it concluded.

The magazine subsequently handed Jon Landau the thankless assignment of reviewing an album that was already receiving massive consumer acceptance. Landau's review concluded that *Blood on the Tracks* was "impermanent" and "would only sound like a great album for a while," opinions that *Rolling Stone* editors would soon supplement with a full-blown tribute to the masterpiece in their very next issue. However, Landau's remains the only *Blood on the Tracks* review still available on the RollingStone.com website and delivers impressions that remain valid twenty-eight years after the release of the album. Landau does not gush over a "comeback" or succumb to the overwhelming tide of critical praise from other camps, instead delivering his own impressions with courageous integrity and brutal honesty. In the end, his begrudging five-star review stands the test of time in much the same way as the album itself.

After using ingenious comparisons with Charlie Chaplin and Elvis Presley to support his contention that Dylan's indifferent approach to recording leaves him a flawed genius, Landau embarks on a lengthy and idiosyncratic assessment of Dylan's recording career vis-à-vis those of his contemporaries, before passing judgment on the album itself.

"The record itself has been made with typical shoddiness," claims Landau. "The accompanying musicians have never sounded more indifferent. The sound is generally no more than . . . a neutral environment from which Dylan emerges. But the singing is much better than on any recent album."

The album's true power, he believes, lies in the writing and Dylan's delivery of his lyrics, producing moments when "he sounds closer, more intimate and more real than anyone else." Landau concludes by listing some of the individual aspects—isolated phrases, inflections, attitudes, and lyrical strategies—that he loves about the album, the most perceptive of which is probably "[Dylan's] extension of the apocalyptic mood of his earlier work into something still forceful, but mellower, more understanding, more tolerant and more self-critical." In summing up, he welcomes *Blood on the Tracks* as an album that, like Dylan himself, "answers to no one and was made for everyone. It is the work of someone who is not just seeing through himself, but looking through us—and still making us see things that we haven't seen before."

In the next issue, following the tremendous sales and public acceptance of *Blood on the Tracks, Rolling Stone* jumped in with both feet, featuring a critics' symposium using the considerable talents of Jon Landau, Paul Williams, Jonathan Cott, Paul Nelson, and others to give the fastest- and best-selling Bob Dylan album to date its due. Paul Nelson declared, "His marriage rumored troubled, his recent tour and albums treated somewhat indifferently by a less than worshipful press, Bob Dylan seems haunted and uncertain again, and that may be very good news," adding on a specifically musical note, "Even the near-anonymous Minneapolis musicians do better than the more gifted but sanctimonious, overrated Band from pseudo-utopian *Planet Waves* days."

Jonathan Cott agreed, claiming that the "clean, gleaming sound" achieved by the Minneapolis musicians "is perfectly suited as a support for Dylan's work." Bud Scoppa joined the chorus, enthusing about the settings and marveling at how "that wonderful, anonymous band has an affinity for Dylan and his music that is clearly poetic."

In his book *Bob Dylan, Performing Artist: The Middle Years,* the always insightful Dylan commentator Paul Williams succinctly places Dylan's musical sidemen in perspective when he observes how "Dylan performs a song not only with his voice but also through the musicians around him; the brilliant success of these Minnesota recordings (and the New York sessions, including most of the discarded tracks, are equally wonderful) is proof again that the power of his presence as a performer can transform whomever [*sic*] is playing with him into a perfect extension of his instincts and his unconscious will. Dylan short-circuits any intellectual approach to music and conducts his bands from his gut, his solar plexus, invisibly, intuitively, trusting the music to find its way into existence if they (he and the band) will just lean into it enough, press through their own limits and surrender to the sound that's trying to happen."

Producer David Z, a Minneapolis native who joined the staff at Sound 80 Studio shortly after the *Blood on the Tracks* sessions, went on to produce hits for Prince, Fine Young Cannibals, and others. Z's views on *Blood on the Tracks* are in concert with Paul Williams's theory about Dylan's extraordinary transformative creative power.

"The best pieces of music are individual captured moments in the lives of a small society known as a musical group," Z believes. "*Blood on the Tracks* is one such piece. The fact that Bob Dylan used a group of relatively unknown musicians, and that he recorded it in a studio in Minneapolis, defines his songs and performances, and helps explain why it is one of his most special-sounding records. Some areas of the country—and the world—have a place where talent has been pent-up and is just waiting for a way to get out. Minneapolis was one such place at that time. By experimenting with recording in his home state, which very few people had done, Dylan used musicians who did not play like anyone that had been heard on records before. Popular music has always been about regional influences, and recordings like this should be cherished as our pop culture becomes increasingly homogenized."

Crawdaddy, the magazine originally founded by Paul Williams, reviewed the album in April. Critic Jim Cusimano, in a piece entitled "Dylan Comes Back to the Wars," found himself very pleasantly surprised that Dylan had "finally found his voice again," following the failures preceding *Blood on the Tracks.* Cusimano posits his theory that the Minneapolis musicians "weren't given much room to work (but listen to the drummer) . . . it rapidly became apparent that Dylan didn't need much help this time around." Thus, Bill Berg's exceptional contributions were duly recognized by the media.

Cusimano joins the virtually unanimous ranks of critics who insist that *Blood on the Tracks* is highly autobiographical. "But even though the biographical facts are extremely illuminating," he believes, "the album is compelling primarily for the ways Dylan exploits them. Although the line between art and life is shaky in Dylan's work, it's still there. The core experience of *Blood on the Tracks* is a man's loss of a beloved woman . . . it's difficult to know whether he's trying to fondle his feelings or purge them." Describing the album as an "emotional roller-coaster," Cusimano reckons that *Blood on the Tracks* succeeds so well "because it projects the pressure of a desperate situation so immediately and realistically that you know the resolution must come from somewhere offstage, beyond vinyl. Against my better judgement, I find myself hoping that she'll take him back. And if *Blood On The Tracks* did that to me, imagine what it did to her."

Despite several extraordinary inaccuracies (such as bestowing credit for the "airy organ chords that accompanied earlier Dylan hits" upon Gregg Inhofer), critic Noe Goldwasser's review in the March 1975 edition of New York's short-lived *ROCK* tabloid contained some pertinent observations. The New York session songs that made the final cut, Goldwasser believes, were "retained for presumably the quality that Eric Weissberg and friends achieved that the Minnesota musicians also seem to have grasped; [the result is] a relaxed, thoughtful album, simple in form, yet growing richer in meaning with every successive listening. . . . I'm glad he coaxed this vision into shape, not remaining satisfied with the imperfect first drafts, as he probably did on *Planet Waves*. I only hope those excised New York sessions don't end up on some future repackaging scheme or another outtakes collection."

It is likely that producer Phil Ramone and Columbia Records, along with legions of Dylan fans, would beg to differ with this last statement. Most of these excised recordings were, in fact, almost immediately made available, appearing a few weeks after *Blood on the Tracks* on a bootleg album called *Joaquin Antique*. Indeed, many "purists" consider the New York versions of the songs found on the Columbia test pressing to be the real McCoy, the "uncut" vision of the artist.

Paul Williams unabashedly loves both the official album *and* the outtakes. "The five New York alternate takes, with the exception of 'Lily,' are classic Dylan performances, very much deserving of release," he enthuses in *Performing Artist,* "even though I believe in each case Dylan was right to choose the later versions, because of the way they contribute to the sound and impact of the album taken as a whole. Our experience of Dylan's art is made richer by our being able to listen to both takes of 'Big Girl,' not just because of what we can learn through the comparison, but because of how much the unchosen take communicates as a performance, how much it gives that is uniquely its own, not to be recaptured at any other moment."

Williams notes that fully a third of "Idiot Wind," in particular, has been rewritten, dispensing with, among other things, yet another stormy image ("We pushed each other a little too far/And one day it just jumped into a raging storm"), but he recognizes that the most striking change is in the *tone* of the performance rather than the actual lyrics. The soft-spoken anger of the earlier version, he contends, may even be more threatening than the furious diatribe of the album version, and you can see his point: Its very reserve casts a sinister shadow over matters treated more cathartically later on.

To some, the changes seemed to suggest Dylan had suddenly developed cold feet about revealing too much of his private life in public, though if that was the case, the alterations did little to dispel the widespread impression that these songs were torn directly from his heart. In March, he all but admitted as much when, in a rare radio interview given to Mary Travers (of Peter, Paul & Mary), he responded peevishly to her comment about how much she enjoyed the new album. "A lot of people tell me they enjoyed that album," he said curtly. "It's hard for me to relate to that—I mean, people enjoying that type of pain . . ."

Apart from alterations to the narrator's aspect—the first three verses being shifted from third person to first person—the main lyrical difference between the two versions of "Tangled Up in Blue" comes in the "Montague Street" verse, which previously included the lines "He was always in a hurry/Too busy or too stoned/And everything that she ever planned/Just had to be postponed." This, along with the more oblique reference to "dealing with slaves" in the later version, notes Williams, "is about as close as Dylan ever gets to acknowledging that he had some substance abuse problems, and that they might have been a factor in his marital difficulties." Indeed, apart from the occasional line here and there—"I took too much for granted, got my signals crossed"; "I can change, I swear"; "I used a little too much force"—the only time Dylan really confronts his own culpability comes, ironically, in the discarded "Up to Me," where he admits his stubbornness, jealousy, and wanderlust are probably at the root of his problems.

Tim Riley, author of *Hard Rain: A Dylan Commentary*, suggests there may be a certain "ironic justice" to the fact that a song as good as "Up to Me" was left off the album. "It shows why Dylan was probably right to chuck the New York tracks for the Minneapolis band," he claims, "not only because with new players the songs get a refreshingly naïve surface that rubs up against their world-weary outlook, but because Dylan's singing in New York is so soft it sounds swallowed." The song's self-referential stance, he believes, nevertheless offers a blueprint for the album's themes of "obsession, denial and melancholy humor."

Dylan's singing on *Blood on the Tracks* also attracted the attention of Paul Williams. "Where is there anyone around today who can sing half this well?" he asked, reviewing the album for the January 30, 1975, edition of the *Soho News*. "I wanted to slug someone at a party recently who was repeating that old canard about Dylan being good in spite of his singing. People don't know what singing is. It's delivery. So-and-so may have a pair of vocal cords that should be put under glass and kept in the Smithsonian; what I want to know is, how much do I hear when that voice speaks to me? Is there an audible, complex consciousness present in the enunciation of every noun, verb and pronoun? When there is, it's not because of the words. Any fool can think, and most can write; *delivering* those thoughts intact to another mind, another consciousness, is

the extraordinary talent. . . . Every word on this record is a
hundred times bigger because of the awareness and skill
with which it is spoken."

"Speaking of idiots," he continues, "I was talking to
some guys the other day who said the musicianship on this
album was not very good. I think they mentioned Mike
Bloomfield as an example of somebody with better musicianship. What a crock. I know these guys; they think musicianship' is measured by how difficult it might be for
somebody else to repeat the same riff. . . . The musicianship
on this album is superb, it couldn't be better, and that's
measurable by the *music* and nothing else. When a song
comes out right, it means everybody was playing great.
When a song comes out right, it's a miracle and we should
be filled with love and fear of God.

"I love this record. Word has it that it was partly
recorded by unknown musicians in Minnesota, and I say
thank the Lord that there are still unknown (and famous)
musicians in this country who can do the right thing at the
right time . . . I happened to hear an earlier recording of this
album, the one done in New York, and the two together sure
taught me a lesson about doing things right and following
hunches and taking chances."

■ ■ ■

Since its release, *Blood on the Tracks* has won an American
Music Award and placed well on various magazines' and
critics' "Best Albums" lists; individual tracks—notably

"Tangled Up in Blue"—have fared equally well on comparable "Best Songs" lists.

It was adjudged twenty-fifth of the *Top 100 Rock'n'Roll
Albums of All Time,* edited by British-American broadcaster
Paul Gambaccini. Acclaiming it in his entry as "a monumen-
tal achievement, cinematic in its scope and epic in its pro-
portions," Niall Stokes of Irish rock magazine *Hot Press*
maintains it "remains the most scarifyingly acute dissection
of marital breakdown ever committed to vinyl."

British rock magazine *Mojo,* including the album in its
house-brick-sized *Mojo Collection* of essential recordings,
considered *Blood on the Tracks* "one of rock's most mature
albums," on which the songwriter was "both more sensitive
and more bitter than he'd been since 1966, [with] a series of
emotionally-charged narratives and reflections that defies
simple assessment." The result, it concludes, is "one of Dylan's most attractive and purely enjoyable albums—an extraordinary achievement, given the often harsh, painful
nature of the subject matter."

Rolling Stone was in broad agreement, claiming in *The
100 Best Albums of the Last 20 Years* that "Dylan seemed
inspired by the complexity of the emotion in a more pro-
found way than ever before," and that the album had "re-
stored Bob Dylan to his standing as a pre-eminent artist."
Ultimately, it concluded, *Blood on the Tracks* is a reflection
on the passing of the 1960s by that decade's greatest pop
icon: "When Dylan sang, with reeling energy, 'There was
music in the cafes at night, and revolution in the air' in
'Tangled Up in Blue,' or concluded that song with a verse

that begins, 'Now I'm going back again, I've got to get to her somehow/All the people we used to know, they're an illusion to me now/Some are mathematicians, some are carpenters' wives/I don't know how it all got started, I don't know what they did with their lives,' it stirred feelings and memories in an entire generation that had been frozen over in the real-life big chill."

TEN

IT IS THANKSGIVING SEASON, 2002. Gregg Inhofer is in perfect voice as he sits at his electric piano at the comfortable Asia Grill in Eden Prairie, Minnesota, opening a set with one of his favorite and most heartfelt songs, "Small Crowds," written by his friend John McAndrew. Inhofer's delivery is sincere and riveting, his plaintive, high tenor voice undiminished by thirty years of gigging in every type of venue, from large halls as part of Olivia Newton-John's touring band to the elite jazz and fusion clubs of the '70s, nightclubs, restaurants, recording studios, and private parties:

> *I like to play for a small crowd*
> *Where I can see your eyes watchin' these songs*
> *And I would rather touch a few very, very, very well in a*
>   *small crowd*
> *I like to play in a dark, smoky room*
> *Where I can hear you well and you can hear me well too*
> *And I would rather touch a few very, very, very well in a*
>   *small crowd.*

It may be just you and I
Is all the crowd there's ever gonna be
But that's enough, oh don't you see, of a crowd for me
An old piano can always be found
And people everywhere they will always gather round
I would rather touch a few very, very well in a small
*   crowd.*
It may be just you and I . . .
I like to play for the small crowd
One at a time, never, ever very loud
And I would rather touch a few very, very, very well in a
*   small crowd.*

Between sets Gregg reflects on his experience with *Blood on the Tracks*.

"I was willing, I guess, to just let bygones be bygones," he says. "I played on a classic album a long time ago and a few people know about it. A friend of mine started sending me pages, three or four years ago, from all these websites showing how many times these songs were released. I was willing to let it all go, but that started to make me think, 'Hey, shouldn't I have some performance royalties on this?' The thing that really hit home was watching VH1's *Top 100 Songs of All Time,* and there it is, number 27, 'Tangled Up in Blue.' I'm on the twenty-seventh top rock hit of all times and I've got nothing to show for it. I don't have a gold record on my wall. I know roadies and soundmen who get gold records from the bands they work with, just because they work with them.

"What I was thinking while I was watching this was what might have happened if we had gotten credit. My career could have been changed. John Farrar, Olivia Newton-John's producer, once told me, 'When you have a hit, money starts coming from every corner of the earth.' He said everybody wants to know what musicians were used, who wrote the song, who produced it, what kind of mikes they used, whether they had Columbian or Peruvian cocaine at the session—they wanted to know everything, so that they could re-create the magic. Especially on an album of that magnitude, which was acclaimed as 'Dylan Has Returned!'"

The experience has clearly left Inhofer with a jaundiced view of the industry in general, and Bob Dylan in particular.

"Any time I hear a Dylan song, whether I played on it or not, it just sticks in my craw and I go, 'Man, what if, what if, what if?'" he reflects bitterly. "Why was I so stupid? Why was I so naïve? But beyond that, I think, even if I was naïve, I was taken advantage of, totally. And I would like to see them make some restitution. I'm not looking for millions of dollars, but it would be nice to go back seven years and get performance royalties. That could change my life at this point.

"At the time, the pay was basic union scale, and I was happy to get it," Inhofer admits. "But I was also promised credits. We were standing, all of the musicians, I think by the door to the control booth in the main studio, and we were shown the album jacket, already pressed, that said

'Eric Weissberg and Deliverance' on it. David Zimmerman made a little speech there along the lines of 'There are a half a million copies of these printed up, and we certainly estimate that it's going to sell out, and on the second printing your names will be credited on the album.' And I was disappointed when it came out and there weren't any. It was only years later that I realized what it could possibly mean to have a credit on an album of that magnitude."

"I believed it," concurs Chris Weber, who also remembers the meeting with David at the door to the control booth. "His brother was a credible source at the time. When we got the album it was obviously *us*, without the credits. There was no excuse that the second and third and fourth pressings, and all the others, weren't updated. Why not? Why didn't they? Is that Jeff Rosen? It's not Bob. Bob couldn't care. It bothered me. It would have been fun. It isn't Bob that stopped us from being on that jacket, is it?"

"It's Bob's noninterference," interjects his spouse, Vanessa.

"But don't you think that on February 12, when the first pressing went gold and sold out, that David or Bob could have made the change?" wonders Weber. "Are we the only ones who weren't credited on a Dylan album? All the people that I cared about in my life knew about it and were proud of me. I think it bothered the other musicians more than it bothered me because they were professionals. I had turned a corner and decided I was not going to be a professional musician anymore; I was going to be a professional businessman and raise a family."

"It's different for Eric Weissberg," believes Weber. "He went in there and recorded a bunch of things with Dylan and, sorry, it didn't work out, except for 'Meet Me in the Morning.' His name is on the album forever. We have a legitimate bitch compared to any unpleasantness Eric went through in the studio. It would be one thing if we'd just had these sessions—and we did have a fun time with him—but if they didn't make the cut, you know, 'Sorry, it didn't work out guys; I'm gonna use these other guys': no problem."

"The difference is that the Minneapolis musicians helped produce a sound that resurrected his career," emphasizes Vanessa Weber. "He needed that punch provided by the Minneapolis bunch to put the album on a whole new playing field."

Gregg Inhofer echoes this sentiment: "If he'd presented material that was charted out and plotted, he could have had hundreds of musicians that could play it equally sufficiently, but he didn't get the results he got until he got the chemistry of the five of us there. That chemistry worked, and as far as recognition goes, that chemistry is worth something."

Chris Weber, however, is resigned to the inaccurate historical record. "It was a disappointment not to see it there in the record stores. If anybody ever questioned it, I had a letter from Zelenovich, *Connie's Insider*, *Rolling Stone*, the *Minnesota Daily*, so I had plenty of proof. But I don't live and breathe and die Bob Dylan. Two or three times a month I go into my basement and I play Bob Dylan songs. I would love to see him again and talk about it, but I don't want to piss him off."

Vanessa Weber believes this would be a highly unlikely possibility, anyway.

"You can't piss off Bob Dylan," she says. "He doesn't care. It's obvious that Bob Dylan wouldn't have gotten where he is without being as self-absorbed as he is. He hasn't ever acknowledged his studio musicians as being as important as they are."

Certainly, following the triple successes of *Blonde on Blonde, John Wesley Harding,* and *Nashville Skyline,* Dylan had withdrawn from the Nashville scene in a similar manner, leaving musicians reeling at how little he had expressed appreciation for their hard work. "I don't think Dylan's ever considered coming back," says veteran Nashville sideman Charlie McCoy, who featured on all three albums, including playing bass and trumpet—simultaneously!—on the hit "Rainy Day Women #12 & 35." Drummer Kenny Buttrey, too, was hurt at the way he and his friends were discarded. "No thank you note . . . no phone calls through the years, no complimentary albums—we had to buy our own," says Buttrey. "That's what's sad."

Vanessa Weber remembers, "Garrison Keillor invited Chris to join the *Prairie Home Companion* [radio show] at that point, because of the Dylan recognition, and was a little bit miffed that Chris didn't want to because he just couldn't do it and run the business at the same time. He recognized Chris's abilities."

"Garrison came into the store," recalls Chris, "which was not uncommon at the time. He wanted a regular band on the show, and he asked me to join. The problem was the show was on Saturdays, and we did three times the business on Saturday that we did on any other day. So I thanked him and told him that would be really neat, but no thanks."

"I would have encouraged it," adds Vanessa. "It would have helped our business to have the continuing credibility of the *Prairie Home Companion* show associated with us. A lot of people, after the sessions, thought that Chris Weber had become rich because he was on Bob Dylan's best-selling album—he was presumed to be Bob Dylan's best friend, and he was supposedly getting all these high residuals. We weren't getting anything. We didn't have any relationship with Bob Dylan, because he walked away from it.

"People would come in and say, 'Congratulations!' and Chris would say, 'Oh, thanks, she's seven pounds, three ounces, and she's twenty-one inches long, and her name is Amanda.' It was just a few days after Amanda was born that the Dylan story leaked, so there was this confusion in our minds about what people were saying. Diehard fans knew about it, but the recognition was never given."

Even David Zimmerman's old classmate Bill Berg, perhaps the most crucial element of the revised versions, admits to "some mild disappointment" at the credits exclusion.

Richard Crooks would also have appreciated something beyond just the collective credit to Eric Weissberg and Deliverance but wasn't overly offended that Dylan rerecorded five of the songs.

"To be honest," he says, "by then I was on to other sessions, and it didn't bother me one way or the other whether he did or didn't—it was his record; he has every right to do whatever he wants with it."

A veteran of countless recording projects, pedal steel guitarist Buddy Cage has few illusions about the way the industry works in this regard.

"It's just typical of record companies not to reprint sleeves," he says. "And it wouldn't have been that much of a big goddamn deal, surely? It's just *printing,* man!" For all that, he remains grateful to Dylan, not just for the chance to play on *Blood on the Tracks,* but in a much wider context.

"Bob Dylan doesn't need an affirmation from me to do what he does naturally as an artist," says Cage. "Most people I talk to about these things, I usually end up saying, 'Look, I don't care what you know and what you don't know, or what you like and what you don't like, but if it weren't for Bob Dylan, we wouldn't be having this conversation right now!' He changed *everything.*"

He doesn't, however, reckon that playing on *Blood on the Tracks* made much difference to his subsequent career.

"I get jobs with other so-called jam bands—be they Dead tribute bands, cover bands, copy bands, whatever—because of my work with The Grateful Dead," he explains, "and I get a lot of work because of the stuff I did with the New Riders, but I frankly can't say that I've ever got work because of being on *Blood on the Tracks.* Usually, I get people saying, 'Holy shit—were you on *that?*'"

Asked whether it was apparent that the songs on *Blood on the Tracks* were about Bob's marriage, Cage is disarming and somewhat coy.

"No, I didn't really put that together at the time," he admits. "I only became a musicologist after the fact—I might have correlated the fact, from *Rolling Stone* or somewhere like that, that Sara had served him notice and stuff. But I didn't put it together at the time. I don't know how he comes up with songs; I know a lot of people try to explain, for whatever reason, what I would consider was the unexplainable. For myself, I have no clue how he gets this stuff. None whatsoever! Bob keeps notes. People say that he has a photographic memory—well, that may be true, but he does keep notes, he's careful about what he does. Like 'Isis'—go figure, y'know? I don't care how you get Bob, if you got it then, or if you get it now—so long as you get it, I'm with you."

Before too long, however, it became impossible for outsiders not to notice that the Dylans' marriage was falling apart, particularly when the songs from *Blood on the Tracks* came to dominate the second leg of the Rolling Thunder Revue the following year. In a retrospective assessment of the *Hard Rain* live album recorded at the revue's penultimate show on May 23, 1976, in Fort Collins, Colorado, John Harris of the British rock magazine *Q* described how Dylan's marital problems had begun to color his interpretations of the *Blood on the Tracks* songs: "Dylan's marriage was hurtling towards termination; he duly dropped most of the material from *Desire* and updated songs from *Blood On the Tracks*, giving them a new vituperative edge. This was the tour-as-soundtrack-to-divorce—art and life colliding, to nobody's great benefit.

"To say that circumstances were less than ideal would be an understatement. A week or so prior to the gig, with Dylan drinking and philandering as if the world was about to end, Sara turned up with their children, demanding to know what he was playing at. As it turned out, imminent divorce was only half the problem. The day of the gig, it was peeing down. Dylan only made things worse by spending the two-day warm-up period in a mountain retreat, getting endlessly drunk.

"After all the dysfunction, Dylan and his band delivered something absolutely incredible. . . . [The *Hard Rain* album contained] nine tracks which flip over countless themes but keep returning to Dylan's marital tear-up. 'Lay Lady Lay,' once a hymn to the love that coursed around the house in Woodstock, receives arguably the cruelest rewrite of all. Now, it's a hymn to the bawdy abandon of drunken adultery. 'Forget this dance,' Dylan yells, 'let's go upstairs! Let's take a chance—who really cares?' If Sara really was waiting in the wings, this was shitty behavior indeed.

"Four songs on, after sounding a note of contrition and self-pity by playing *Nashville Skyline*'s 'I Threw It All Away'—delivered in a veritable howl—the record closes with 'Idiot Wind.' This is vicious: its spite is balanced by regret on *Blood On The Tracks*' setting, but here it's allowed to mutate into something almost wholly hateful. 'Visions of your chestnut mare' becomes 'visions of your smoking tongue.' [But it is the Clash-style reggae reading of] 'Shelter From The Storm'—featuring hands-of-concrete slide guitar—that exercises the most addictive spell. It is, quite simply, one of the most exciting things he has ever recorded—proof that his endless re-tooling of his songs can result in completely fresh inventions, and that strife and discord are often great music's meat and drink. 'It was,' Dylan surmised, 'like a punk record or something.'"

Unlike most of the other musicians on *Blood on the Tracks*, Buddy Cage remained in contact with Dylan for several years afterward.

"Later on, Dylan got close to Garcia," he confides. "I wouldn't presume to tell you what their relationship was, how much Bob thought of Jerry, and how much Jerry thought of Bob. But it was really dynamic: Bob came all the way out to Marin County to see if he and the band could fit in with each other, play together. This was from about '82 to about '88 or something like that. They kept it up for a while, and it was always very weird: The Dead were always conscious of just who Bob was, his importance, and they couldn't, to my mind, quite get a grip on how to play his stuff. It was a really strange deal: Bob, I know, got involved with what Jerry was doing, drug-wise—that's my take on it—until finally Dylan kind of went, 'Whoa! Boy, if I keep this up I'm gonna be dead in a year!' I think he probably came to that conclusion, and he quit everything."

Around this time, Cage got to attend some of the rehearsals for the Dylan & The Dead tour, at the band's Bay Area studio space.

"At The Dead's warehouse, half the place was studio, and the other half was equipment storage," he explains. "Mickey Hart had just spent months doing stuff for *Apoca-*

lypse Now, all these tracks, and they had given him all these monitors—when you walked into the studio, there were, like, ten Sony Trinitrons lying around the place, on the console and everywhere, and at one end of the studio there were these three tympani drums surrounded by these huge gongs, four or five feet in diameter, in a circle around that, and then in a circle around that were all these fifty-six-inch projection screens that Hart was using to do his tracks against. I can remember everybody waiting for Dylan to get there, and when he walked in with his guitar, he took one look at it, turned around, and walked straight back out to the parking lot.

"Garcia had to follow him and find out what was wrong. When he got out there, Bob said, 'Get them fuckin' TV sets out of there, man!' and Jerry said, 'Bob, they're not even plugged in—we haven't used them for years!' Bob said, 'I don't give a shit—it's my publishing.' Bob is, like, really nuts about that, because he's been bootlegged so many times. So we had to remove them, take them all over to the other side of the warehouse, and after that everything was cool. It was fun to watch all this going on."

Buddy, who went on to play with the re-formed lineup of The Band in the '80s and '90s, remains a staunch advocate of Dylan, as does his young spouse.

"My wife just turned thirty-one," he says, "and she listens to *Blood on the Tracks*. She's a Deadhead, but a young one—a retro Deadhead, if you like! She was at a Dead show when they were working with Dylan, and Scully [Rock Scully, former Grateful Dead manager], who knew her, popped her into a room backstage. There was one other person in the room—Dylan. She looked at him and said, 'Oh, I know you!,' and he said, 'Oh, yeah? Well, I don't know *you!*' and they got to talking. She hit it off with Bob, and they moved over to Garcia's dressing-room—between the three of them, they probably had a spiritual moment, of whatever kind!"

There's no question, however, of her priorities: "She got a big kick out of it, being able to meet Jerry before he died."

Like Buddy, Eric Weissberg doesn't believe his association with Dylan has had much of an effect one way or the other on his subsequent workload.

"I don't think playing on *Blood on the Tracks* made any difference to my career," he reckons, "as I have gone on to be involved in several thousand other sessions over the decades."

Deliverance drummer Richard Crooks feels the opportunity to work with Dylan may have been slightly beneficial for his career, but not noticeably so.

"As far as people knowing I played on *Blood on the Tracks*—though it was only by word of mouth that that information was passed around—it didn't hurt," he admits. "It was a little mark on your side of the line. If my name had been attached to it, it might have made more of a difference—but again, that and a buck seventy-five'll still get you downtown on the subway!"

Crooks is more interested in the here and now, remaining active on a variety of fronts. He even worked with Dylan again just a few years ago, on secretive sessions recorded in

Chicago with guitarist David Bromberg, who had previously played on Dylan's *Self Portrait* album.

"It was funny," he recalls of Bob's presence. "It's like, the middle of June in Chicago, 100 degrees and 99 percent humidity, and it's not raining, and this guy's walking around in double-thick Levis with engineer boots, a T-shirt, a hooded sweatshirt, and a barn jacket, with these dark glasses on. Everybody else is almost naked! He was trying to be, like, incognito!"

Despite his initial annoyance at having his work on *Blood on the Tracks* replaced, Deliverance guitarist Charlie Brown is fine with the way things turned out.

"I don't have any bad feelings about it at all, just good feelings," he concedes. "I'm glad we did it, and I wish we could have done more—but hey, that's the way it goes!

"I didn't realize how much attention there was on this record until recently," he adds.

When Bill Berg hears something from the Minneapolis sessions on the radio, he feels the warm glow of a job well done.

"We sound good," he contends. "It makes me refocus on the significance of those few days. Every time I hear 'Tangled Up in Blue' or 'Idiot Wind,' I am reminded that this guy meant business; he *knew* what he wanted. For me, it was a lesson in blind commitment to a project. Listening to Dylan's count-off through the headphones, watching him in the rapture of his performance—these are the memories it stirs up in me that I'll never be able to describe."

Berg also feels he has one of the answers as to why Dylan rerecorded five of the songs.

"We were more cohesive than the New York cats, just because of our experience together, and with Kottke," he believes. "Billy and I instantly tuned into what Dylan wanted, and we gave it to him. He knew it, we knew it. It *rocks*, period." Nor is he wishy-washy about his feelings for the finished product: "It is a better record because Bob knew he had to go for something more, and he did. Dylan made all the right decisions, right up to the mastering."

Minneapolis engineer Paul Martinson, too, had fun. "I was hard at work on this, yet there was a sense of enjoyment for me," he recalls, "particularly at the second session because the nerves weren't there. Here's a major star in the studio and you want to make sure he likes it. I felt that 'Idiot Wind' was a major piece of writing, with as much poetry and imagery as anything since John Milton. 'Tangled Up in Blue' and 'Lily, Rosemary and the Jack of Hearts' are two of my favorite songs that Dylan has ever done. They were lots of fun to record. I still think it holds up pretty well."

Charlie Brown believes "What we played was certainly disposable, but we had fun doing it, and whenever we got the chance to do a record, like *Blood on the Tracks*, it was such a treat—we got to play with a human being!" But it's hard for even a legend like Bob Dylan to impress a seasoned session player like Charlie: "That Streisand album I did went platinum in *one week*—that shows *her* power!"

Only pianist Tom McFaul, from the New York sessions, downplays the significance of his own participation in *Blood on the Tracks*. "I've never thought it fair to try to publicize my involvement in a project I had so little to do with and made such a minor contribution to, if any," he claims modestly. "Playing on *Blood on the Tracks* had no effect on my career. I still haven't heard the album. Maybe now I should finally listen to it."

Not, McFaul is quick to point out, that this should be taken as inferring he has a low regard for Dylan's work. Quite the contrary.

"I have always greatly admired Bob Dylan's music," he maintains. "I think the first album I really listened to was *Another Side of Bob Dylan,* back in college. He is a master of language and almost always finds a unique and fitting way of expressing himself musically. He has never been stuck in one place but, rather like other great artists, is always growing. His influence on all pop music is vast and unquestionable. Though he started in rock, adapted folk elements in his music, then went back to rock, he is really sui generis. His songs and style are inimitable. When I say I have not listened to *Blood on the Tracks,* it is not intended as a smug remark from some pretend jaded studio musician; it is, for whatever reason, simply the truth."

For Eric Weissberg, the experience has not, he insists, soured his opinion of Dylan, whom he bumps into now and again around town.

"I have met Bob on the street in midtown New York a couple of times, and he has always been most gracious and complimentary, and I love him for that, too," he says, adding, "I would love to be playing with him now. But perhaps if we had done the whole album, and he loved it, we would have gone out with him, and lots could have been different with that course of history. But I don't regret it not happening that way at all."

Chris Weber's favorite story about the impact of *Blood on the Tracks* came out of a few drinks at a marina bar. "I was out once with my brother on his boat in Chesapeake Bay," he says. "So we pull into the dock at the Annapolis Marina, shower, and go into the local pub, and there was this band playing, and they were good. They've really got it. They're playing Neil Young and all this kind of great stuff, and we're havin' a few beers. At one point there was a lull and I yell out, 'Do you know any Dylan?' And what do they do?—Of all the songs they could have done, there it was, 'Tangled Up in Blue.' That surprised me."

"Bob Dylan created a Camelot," believes Vanessa Weber. "In Bob Dylan's eyes, he has created himself as the sole person creating everything that he has written and done, and he's the King Arthur of his own court. It's a dysfunc tional Camelot. He doesn't want to give credit to David, to his musicians, to anybody else. In his own mind, everything that Bob Dylan has got out there is the sole product of Bob Dylan, and he doesn't care to admit to the fact that somebody else may have had something to do with creating that persona."

True enough, the musicians' credits on all subsequent pressings and formats of *Blood on the Tracks* have never been updated. Eric Weissberg and Deliverance played wonderfully on "Meet Me in the Morning" on the official release, yet with few exceptions, the musicians have never received a note of thanks, a phone call, or complimentary copies of records or, as is considered a common industry courtesy with successful projects, received RIAA sales awards of gold or platinum disks. Yet a single phone call from Jeff Rosen in Dylan's New York office to Columbia Records, and the Recording Industry Association of America would issue the awards at nominal cost to Dylan.

Sizing up the effect the Dylan sessions had on his career, Tony Brown is succinct. "It was a great experience. It didn't hurt. I knew some guys beforehand who grew more interested in my material after the sessions. And a lot of folkies wanted me to play with them after that." Brown eventually moved away from playing music altogether, developing a successful career designing home accessories with his wife's company, Babette Holland Design. Organist Paul Griffin has died; he was a major contributor to sessions from "Like a Rolling Stone" to the haunting organ glissandos heard in the superb New York outtakes of "Idiot Wind." And although their relationship warmed up immediately upon the enormous success of *Blood on the Tracks*, Dylan still chooses not to publicly recognize his brother, who enabled him to achieve his marvelous vision.

It is no mystery that David remains relatively tight-lipped about his brother's activities. Family businesses are not always easy to manage, but Bob and David are trusting business partners in an extremely lucrative string of enterprises. Although it must have been incredibly difficult for David to live in the shadow of the most famous musician on the planet, *Blood on the Tracks* ensured his permanent departure from his day job as a music teacher in the northwest suburbs of Minneapolis and paved the way for a closeness and undying loyalty between the brothers, born of absolute necessity. Blood, as they say, is thicker than water, and Bob's latest success was creating new challenges to his family life and privacy. He needed a bulwark against intrusions, someone he could trust implicitly, and so David was taken on to manage Bob's every move while he was living on The Farm in Minnesota.

"It was sad for David, who was like two different people," says Ellen Steinman, who was David's business supervisor in the years following *Blood on the Tracks*. "One when Bob was not around and another when Bob was there. He'd go from confident, warm, and gracious David to subservient, cowering little boy. The deal was that during the summer, when Bob was here, I couldn't call David when Bob was in town. Sometimes I'd have to call, because I was twenty-something years old and running their theater [the Orpheum, in Minneapolis], and David would pretend to be talking to the cleaners or something, and I would know Bob was nearby. It was very strange.

"What a drag, to be hostage in your home! What a life! David was at his beck and call when Bob was here and would call me to go and do things. For instance, he would say, 'Bob needs a manual typewriter. Go find it and bring it out here.' It wasn't that easy to find a brand new manual typewriter with certain specifications. So I'd find it and run it out there and he'd say, 'Oh, Bob won't use this; it isn't American-made.' It had to be there in two hours, and then, you know, it wasn't the right one. Then it was 'Bob wants Earth Shoes.' Remember Earth Shoes, hanging upside down from the ceiling? David would call me during the summer to execute Bob's whims."

Steinman became a trusted part of the Dylan organization (Minneapolis branch) and was given the Orpheum Theater to run when the original management company in Seattle disappeared into thin air with the box office proceeds, leaving several unpaid bills.

"Bob didn't want to put any money into the theater," she recalls. "He'd pay the liquor license and the property taxes because he owned the building, but that was it. Anything that happened there, we had to make the money and spend the money that we made. Bob's sons, Jakob and Sam, used to work concessions at the Orpheum in the summers, and his stepdaughter, Maria, worked in the box office.

"A local journalist named Marty Keller found out that Bob's daughter was working at the theater, and he was going to write a story about Bob. He started hanging out and coming to shows, and eventually he met Maria. He was cute and he flirted with Maria, and of course, his ultimate goal was to meet Bob. It got to that point where they were going out, and they got to the house and he meets Bob. Then it transpired that he really just wanted to write this story, and of course Maria was ready to never speak to another male in her life. She already thought everybody just dated her to meet her father anyway, but Marty took it to the max. He managed to date her until he got out to the house to meet Bob. He was on the shit list from that point forward."

The pecking order at The Farm extended, Steinman claims, to the two brothers' children.

"David's kids, when Bob's kids were here, also became a secondary priority," she says. "Suddenly, David didn't talk about his own kids in the summer when Bob's kids were here. So now it was Jesse and Maria and Jakob and Sam, and I had to employ everybody. David would refer to Bob and his kids almost as if they were like gods. And then it was 'The Farm,' not 'going over to my uncle's house' or 'going home.' David lived there and his kids lived there, but during the summer it was, like, 'Well, we'll be at THE FARM.' Every time someone said it we'd laugh and say, 'Okay, let's go to THE FARM.' It started to sound bizarre. There was a change in their voice inflection, in the way they would say THE FARM. The dynamics, everything would change during the summer when Bob's kids were here. It wasn't 'My nephews' anymore, it became 'Bob's kids.' It was weird. We all thought it was weird. We used to call it Southfork, because everybody had their own house on the property, and the art studio, the music studio, the gym, the guest houses— Beatty's guest house; Gail's mother had a house.

"I always found the relationship between the brothers depressing. When Bob was in town in the summer, every time he wanted to do something it had to be orchestrated. David would be orchestrating how Bob's gonna go to a Twins game, which he loved to do. Or he was going to come to a show—which I thought was hysterical, because everybody's inside, and he would go up and sit in the balcony, and yet he would feel a need, when he walked through the empty lobby, to cover his face! This was like when Prince would come, and they'd say, 'We don't want anybody to know he's there.' But Prince would come after everybody in the audience was seated, through a side door with body-guards, dressed in a purple cape! If he'd just walked in nor-mally, nobody would know he was there! Bob would do the same thing."

Steinman grew to understand and accommodate the changed dynamic of life at The Farm, especially the way it affected David's attitude.

"You're either David's friend, and that's it, or once you're trying to get to know something, or to get information about Bob, you become one of the masses of people out in the world who do that," she explains. "You're only as solid as when you're 'in the club.' If you're looking for any infor-mation on David's brother, anything about Bob, you're sud-denly out of the club. He's molded his life on protecting Bob."

Indeed, David "circled the wagons" around the immedi-ate family and business operatives on learning about this book project. But then, who could blame *anyone* in the Dy-lan camp for being protective?

"I should write a book!" responded David over lunch with one of the authors at Dobo's Café in June 2002, on hearing the news that this project was in motion. But it was a moot point. Both parties knew he couldn't, and wouldn't, ever write a book about his famous brother. Certainly, there can be no blanket trust extended to any quarter of the fourth estate, regardless of past associations, in the wake of the new crop of sensational exposés purporting to air the laundry of America's greatest troubadour.

"We had, in the safe, three or four FBI files on weirdos," says Ellen Steinman, who developed a keen appreciation of the pressures that celebrity bestows on a star's personal life. "There was a girl that had been stalking him, who had legally changed her name to Carmella Dylan. She actually would show up on tours, call ahead, and cancel everything! She was very believable. She'd make plans, book hotel rooms, and so forth. Then they would get there and the promoters would say, 'Well, your wife called, you know, Carmella Dylan,' and they would know what had happened. She was a stalker, but she also did all this weird stuff and got away with it. This scared me, because I thought she would, like the John Lennon thing, you know, come in and kill everybody.

"'Carmella' called up writer Bob Protzman at the *St. Paul Pioneer Press* one time and said, 'This is Carmella Dylan, I'm going to be here a few days. Can I stay at your apartment?' So he gave her a key to his apartment and let her stay there! Then she went to a dance company and took lessons and said, 'Bob will pay for it,' and people were falling for it! She was completely believable. She stole everything she could from Protzman within the week she was in town. Then David planted an item in the newspaper that said Bob had left for two weeks in Jamaica, and sure enough, she bought a ticket, and they followed her and caught her by the ticket counter.

"They came to know when something was happening with one of these people. Somebody broke into the Orpheum Theater and broke into the pop machine and then into my desk, looking for the address or phone number for The Farm. There was one guy who was getting out of prison, and they had to watch these people all the time." In an industry where personal privacy is the exception to the rule, the Dylan camp has become, through trial and error, a model of controlled restraint.

And who was the architect of this model? Was it David Zimmerman, who has served his brother faithfully throughout his career? Jeff Rosen, custodian of Dylan's copyrights, who thwarts most requests for interviews and information without so much as a response? No, it is Bob Dylan himself who defines and controls his universe.

Dylan learned hard lessons from his early associations with Albert Grossman and the music publishers who held on to his copyrights throughout his early career. When Jeff Rosen's predecessor, Naomi Saltzman, and attorney David Braun found that all was not right with the ownership of Dylan's copyrights and catalog, the chain of events was triggered that propelled Rosen into his guardian status, a position he does not take lightly. He is only occasionally overruled by Dylan himself, as when journalist Paul Zollo successfully approached publicist Elliot Mintz for arguably one of the best Dylan interviews ever published, in *SongTalk* magazine, reprinted in the newest edition of Zollo's *Songwriters on Songwriting*. It is Dylan himself who was always interested in a deal that worked. It is Dylan who has always had journalists eating out of the palm of his hand, waiting for his next "unauthorized" exclusive interview.

"Dylan's insecurity shows up in his writings," believes Vanessa Weber. "You have to have some level of insecurity because of the sensitivity required to produce what he has produced, and you have to have a high level of insecurity not to share some of the glory. Look at Richard Nixon: Mr. Insecurity. Do you think that he had any kind of belief that he should give credit to somebody else for something that Richard Nixon did? Bob Dylan felt that at the same time as Richard Nixon and didn't want to diminish his own persona. Dylan is revealing himself to be unconsciously Nixonian. He recognized in Nixon that sole person who's out there on this island and has to, by God, protect everything he's got. Dylan maintains his island to this day. He's afraid of the sharks. Everybody's a shark. You have to be a megalomaniac to reach the level that he has."

Although these comments reflect a bitter cynicism, they are corroborated by Dylan's 1975 Paris roommate, David Oppenheim, with whom he stayed after the release of *Blood on the Tracks*. "Dylan is a bloke who invents everything," said Oppenheim. "He's the most egotistical person I know. That's what makes him an incredible person, his amazing self-confidence . . . he stripped me of all my ideas of wealth, of fame, or romanticism and love."

"Your corrupt ways had finally made you blind," sings Bob Dylan in "Idiot Wind." This could have referred to Dylan's first manager, Albert Grossman; to disgraced President Nixon (it was written on the eve of Nixon's resignation); or to Dylan himself. Most likely, as Dylan has tried to explain a thousand times in interviews, it is a composite, an invented character, a literary device to tell a story. No emotion attached? That's arguable and, in view of the actual chain of events leading to Dylan's divorce, doubtful.

After Paul Martinson sent the masters for the five Minneapolis songs off to L.A. for mastering, the New York bootlegs went into wide circulation almost immediately, along with outtakes of the early Minneapolis rehearsals of "Idiot Wind." Dylan has been the prime prey for bootleggers ever since the *Great White Wonder* double album of *Basement Tapes* and early '60s Minneapolis recordings became illicitly available in 1968. Indeed, during a legal dispute between Dylan and his former tour manager, Victor Maymudes, in 1998, RIAA official Frank Creighton affirmed in court that Dylan was "probably the most bootlegged artist in the history of the music industry"—a situation that had by then caused the singer to adopt more assertive security measures to guard his copyrights and archive materials.

Despite his efforts, the bootlegs continue to appear, seeping out of all manner of sources; one tape was even filched from the U.S. Copyright Office, and as musician Charlie Daniels told biographer Howard Sounes, recordings from the Dylan/George Harrison sessions for *New Morning,* on which Daniels played, mysteriously appeared despite all parties' stringent security measures. "I could never figure out how Dylan's stuff was so easily bootlegged," Daniels said, explaining that although he personally delivered the master tapes to Dylan's office following each session, "Still it would get bootlegged!" Likewise, *Blood on the Tracks* outtakes from both

A&R Studios in New York and Sound 80 Studio in Minneapolis somehow found their way into the record racks.

For all Dylan's professed annoyance about bootleggers, it still remains possible to purchase, mere weeks after the performances, bootlegs of virtually every concert—and we're not talking about furtive, lo-fi cassette recordings snatched by members of the audience, either; we're talking about beautifully mixed recordings of such impeccable sound quality that they could only have derived from a soundboard (mixing desk) feed. How the bootleggers get access to the desk remains a mystery, but it is hard not to suspect that, if not actively condoning them like his friends in The Grateful Dead, Dylan may have been forced to turn a blind eye to practices he publicly condemns.

Phil Ramone, who was sound engineer on huge tours by the likes of Paul Simon, as well as Dylan and The Band's 1974 Before the Flood jaunt, still marvels at the bootleggers' persistence. "If we played Santa Monica Civic Auditorium with Paul Simon, or whoever I was touring with, I could go to a little store on Sunset and buy the cassette of the show days later," he admits. One possible source, he reveals, may be the individual venues' public address systems. "I was conscious of the house feed—because you have to give a house feed to the main control room, so they could feed the dressing rooms and/or the management, as they used to say. Besides that, I would walk through the auditorium and see guys with little Nagra tape machines and a big hat, and inside the sombrero would be the mikes—you've never seen rigs like these!

"Funnily enough," he adds, "[concert bootlegging] didn't start with pop and rock; it started with opera. I know people who'd say, 'We have Pavarotti in '72 at the Met,' and another would respond, 'Yes, but I have the third night, when he does *Il Trovatore*'! It's an amazing group of people who do that."

With regard specifically to the bootlegs of *Blood on the Tracks* material, Ramone remains bemused—though not really surprised—that his usual stringent precautions failed to prevent the outtakes' becoming available.

"I'm always anxious to know how [they appeared]," he muses, "because I thought I had pretty good control over the stuff! But I realized that once the tapes went over to Columbia, anybody had a chance to copy them."

Ironically, Ramone found that the *Blood on the Tracks* outtakes bootleg came in handy when he was commissioned to remaster the album for 5.1 surround sound, as part of the recent ambitious SACD reissue program of Dylan's back catalog.

"Truthfully, I had to go out and buy a bootleg three months before the remastering," he admits, "just to hear how the bootlegs were. This newspaperman called me and said, 'I know you're doing this, and I'm in love with the Dylan world, and *Blood on the Tracks* has been the one that's always kept as a mystery.' I don't think Bob wants it kept as a mystery—unless there's something awful that we shouldn't know about!—because as your career goes on, it's important to hear it as it was, about the truth of the relationship."

Ramone's task was hampered by the difficulties in locating the original master tapes of some of the songs.

"There were five songs missing from the multitrack," he reveals. "They could find the two-track, but not the multi-track. Bob's company has control of everything in his life now, and when they finally found the tapes, they had been misfiled under some 'Extra Miscellaneous' file or something. When they showed up, it was as if they'd just been put away, with the take sheets and everything."

Thanks to the fragile nature of the medium, the remastering process was a lot more convoluted than it might have been. "We had to bake [the tapes] for a day," Ramone explains, "because the tapes of the '70s, compared to the '60s, I guess the backing was changed, and it has a tendency to possibly shed, so you have to bake them carefully for twelve hours and let them cool down slowly for twelve hours. Then we transferred them all to a digital format, very carefully. Because I was an engineer most of my life, I know the pitfalls of transference in tape. Things get tampered with when they get digitized, and they don't always get better." As Ramone was listening to the newly recovered master tapes, Sony executive Steve Berkowitz dropped by the studio and was struck by the clarity of the original recordings. "He said, 'God, that's warm and round; what a different sound,'" recalls Ramone, "and I said, 'Well, somebody decided to add more high end to his voice and things during the original transfer from analogue to CD.'"

The remastering gave Ramone the chance to restore *Blood on the Tracks* to its original (pre-CD) condition, taking care to retain its simplicity and immediacy. The new 5.1

surround-sound mix, meanwhile, afforded him the opportunity to try out something new, without materially affecting the original recordings.

"There's an approach that some people have, which I find somewhat restrictive, in thinking that the surround mix should be done from the tenth row, center," he explains. "I decided instead that I would put the audience in the room with Bob, kind of like the way he sits and stands and relates to his bass player. On some cuts, which I think is unique in surround sound, there's just bass and guitar and Bob's voice.

"When you make albums, they age with you," Ramone reflects. "Very seldom do you get the chance to take them apart again. They're like time capsules—when you live it, it's part of your life, and it goes on and you move on, and you know the artists from different times and places. But when something becomes a landmark in [an artist's] career, you say to yourself, 'Well, I was happy to be a part of it.' I was surprised at some of the things I'd done. I was happy with some of it, but you're always questioning why you do things. But I think from a technical and a musical point of view, the immediacy is what I loved and remembered about the album."

The immediacy and simplicity were stringently protected, with no attempt made to update or rerecord any of the parts, or to significantly alter the original stereo mix.

"I could have, but there's a certain history you don't need to touch," affirms Ramone. "It's like colorizing a black-and-white picture. And I just wouldn't do that to Dylan. I might have to see him on the street some day, and he's either going to give you the thumbs up, or he's going to look at you with a scowl, and I don't need that!"

■ ■ ■

Bill Berg did eventually crank the ignition of his white Volvo station wagon and move to Los Angeles, where he became a top animator at Disney, going on to draw the "Hades" character in *Hercules* and the Beast in *Beauty and the Beast.* Berg's final credits for Disney included the character drawings for Long John Silver in *Treasure Planet* and three "dumb and dumber"–type characters for *Home on the Range.* He feels proud of being a part of the generation of filmmakers who "fused digital animation with traditional animation." Berg retired from the Walt Disney animation department in 2003, hoping to continue his association with the Wayne Johnson Quintet, reconnect with musicians, write new music, and dedicate his career to playing jazz.

Billy Peterson remains active as a touring and studio musician, record producer, and club owner. Following the sessions for *Blood on the Tracks,* producer David Rivkin (soon to become Prince's engineer/producer David Z) introduced Billy to renowned musician and musicologist Ben Sidran, who in turn introduced Billy to his employer for the next fifteen years, Steve Miller. Peterson co-owns The Artists Quarter jazz club in St. Paul, Minnesota, and remains an in-demand bassist and record producer with an international reputation and following.

After a highly successful career as head of a music production company supplying advertising jingles and music for
commercials, Tom McFaul now spends most of his time
composing and producing classical music. "I recently completed my Mass in C Minor, for five soloists, chorus, and orchestra," he says, eagerly anticipating the piece's world
premiere performance. "Recently I produced the debut CD
from The Fry Street Quartet, recordings of Beethoven's Op.
59, No. 3, and the Janacek First String Quartet, by this fine
young string quartet who made their Carnegie Hall debut
last year. I am currently writing a string quartet myself and
finishing a set of solo piano pieces."

Chris and Vanessa Weber sold The Podium Guitar Shop
in 1985 and became successful realtors in Minnetonka, Minnesota. The Webers turned their home into a rehearsal studio for the 2001 reunion of the *Blood on the Tracks*
Minneapolis house band, which played to a packed house at
First Avenue (a large downtown club that was the primary
location for Prince's movie *Purple Rain*) to headline Paul
Metsa's raucous celebration of Bob Dylan's sixtieth birthday.

Kevin Odegard still plays and sings regularly and is a frequent contributor to trade and consumer publications.

Mandolinist/composer Peter Ostroushko is a best-selling
recording artist on the Red House label, a regular guest
artist on Garrison Keillor's *Prairie Home Companion,* and a
very popular touring performer.

Paul Martinson is "somewhat retired" and living in
South Minneapolis. He consults for Trail Mix Studios.

Eric Weissberg lives in upstate New York in a house once owned by his idol and mentor, Pete Seeger. Eric continues to play concerts and recording dates and recently completed a long run with Art Garfunkel's touring band. Charlie Brown remains active in the business, as does drummer Richard Crooks, who has worked recently with Larry Campbell and Tony Garnier (guitarist and bassist, respectively, with Dylan's present top-notch touring band) on an album for Soozie Tyrell, the violin player in Bruce Springsteen's band.

"Tony and Larry and I were doing a session last week," Crooks reveals, "and they were talking about how much better and more organized [Dylan] was getting, but they said there were still moments when they realized he'd never played a part that way before—he still kept them guessing! But what a memory this guy has—all those songs he's written, with all those verses, and he never uses a cheat sheet, nothing like that; it all just comes falling out. So who cares if he adds an extra bar here or there? He's always reaching for something a little different, a bit better."

Phil Ramone remains active as one of the most versatile and sought-after producers in the music industry, equally at home supervising the music for the Grammy Awards telecast or producing albums for any number of A-list artists. In such high demand is Ramone that at one point in 1980 he found himself producing albums simultaneously for Billy Joel, Paul Simon, and Stephanie Mills, working around the clock at A&R Studios, which he then owned.

As for Bob Dylan, well, he's still on the road, heading for another joint. Though now in his sixties, he keeps up a concert schedule that shames rock stars half his age, drawing audiences of all ages to hundreds of sell-out shows each year around the world. After a period treading water through much of the '90s, he has reemerged in recent years with two of the finest albums of his career, *Time Out of Mind* and *Love and Theft,* which have secured his best reviews (and sales) since *Blood on the Tracks.* His work is a cornerstone of our culture and will remain a literary watermark for the many generations he has already touched, and for the thousands of younger devotees who get bitten by the Dylan "bug" each year. His influence and prominence as a songwriter, poet, and performer will never fade. His songs will always be sung, and his prophecies will continue to ring true.

CUE SHEETS

ACCORDING TO MICHAEL KROGSGAARD'S Scandinavian Institute for Rock Research, which has had the most extensive access to the session documentation, the studio logs for the New York sessions might have looked something like this:

SEPTEMBER 16, STUDIO A, A&R RECORDING, NEW YORK CITY

 1 If You See Her, Say Hello
 2 If You See Her, Say Hello—*The Bootleg Series, Vols. 1–3*
 3 You're a Big Girl Now
 4 You're a Big Girl Now
 5 Simple Twist of Fate
 6 Simple Twist of Fate
 7 You're a Big Girl, Now
 8 Up to Me
 9 Lily, Rosemary and the Jack of Hearts
10 Simple Twist of Fate
11 Simple Twist of Fate
12 Simple Twist of Fate

13 Call Letter Blues
14 Meet Me in the Morning—released on *BOTT*
15 Call Letter Blues—*The Bootleg Series, Vols. 1–3*
16 Idiot Wind
17 Idiot Wind
18 Idiot Wind
19 Idiot Wind
20 Idiot Wind
21 Idiot Wind
22 You're Gonna Make Me Lonesome When You Go
23 You're Gonna Make Me Lonesome When You Go
24 You're Gonna Make Me Lonesome When You Go
25 You're Gonna Make Me Lonesome When You Go
26 You're Gonna Make Me Lonesome When You Go
27 You're Gonna Make Me Lonesome When You Go
28 You're Gonna Make Me Lonesome When You Go
29 You're Gonna Make Me Lonesome When You Go
30 Tangled Up in Blue—*The Bootleg Series, Vols. 1–3*

SEPTEMBER 17, STUDIO A, A&R RECORDING, NEW YORK CITY

1 You're a Big Girl Now
2 You're a Big Girl Now—*Biograph*
3 Tangled Up in Blue
4 unknown
5 Blues jam
6 You're Gonna Make Me Lonesome When You Go
7 Shelter from the Storm
8 Shelter from the Storm

9 Buckets of Rain

10 Tangled Up in Blue

11 Buckets of Rain

12 Shelter from the Storm—released on soundtrack to *Jerry Maguire*, 1996

13 Shelter from the Storm (fast)

14 Shelter from the Storm—released on *BOTT*

15 You're Gonna Make Me Lonesome When You Go

16 You're Gonna Make Me Lonesome When You Go—released on *BOTT*

SEPTEMBER 19, STUDIO A, A&R RECORDING, NEW YORK CITY

1 Up to Me

2 Up to Me

3 Buckets of Rain

4 Buckets of Rain

5 Buckets of Rain

6 Buckets of Rain—released on *BOTT*

7 If You See Her, Say Hello

8 Up to Me

9 Up to Me

10 Up to Me

11 Meet Me in the Morning

12 Meet Me in the Morning

13 Buckets of Rain

14 Tangled Up in Blue

15 Tangled Up in Blue

16 Tangled Up in Blue

17 Simple Twist of Fate
18 Simple Twist of Fate
19 Simple Twist of Fate—released on *BOTT*
20 Up to Me
21 Up to Me—*Biograph*
22 Idiot Wind
23 Idiot Wind
24 Idiot Wind
25 Idiot Wind—*The Bootleg Series, Vols. 1–3*
26 You're a Big Girl Now
27 Meet Me in the Morning
28 Meet Me in the Morning
29 Meet Me in the Morning
30 Meet Me in the Morning
31 Meet Me in the Morning
32 Meet Me in the Morning
33 Tangled Up in Blue
34 Tangled Up in Blue
35 Tangled Up in Blue

SEPTEMBER 24, STUDIO A, A&R RECORDING, NEW YORK CITY

1 Meet Me in the Morning
2 Meet Me in the Morning
3 Meet Me in the Morning
4 Meet Me in the Morning
5 Meet Me in the Morning
6 Meet Me in the Morning
7 Meet Me in the Morning—released on *BOTT*

8 Call Letter Blues—*The Bootleg Series, Vols. 1–3*

9 You're a Big Girl Now—*Biograph*

10 Tangled Up in Blue (?)

11 Idiot Wind

Overdubs: Buddy Cage, steel guitar

DECEMBER 27, SOUND 80, MINNEAPOLIS, MINNESOTA

1 Idiot Wind (rehearsal)

2 Idiot Wind

3 Idiot Wind

4 Idiot Wind

5 Idiot Wind—released on *BOTT*

6 You're a Big Girl Now

7 You're a Big Girl Now—released on *BOTT*

Overdubs: Bob Dylan, Hammond B-3 organ (Idiot Wind); guitar (You're a Big Girl Now); vocal punch-ins (Idiot Wind)

DECEMBER 30, SOUND 80, MINNEAPOLIS, MINNESOTA

1 Tangled Up in Blue (G version)

2 Tangled Up in Blue (partial A version, rehearsal)

3 Tangled Up in Blue—released on *BOTT*

4 Lily, Rosemary and the Jack of Hearts (rehearsal)

5 Lily, Rosemary and the Jack of Hearts—released on *BOTT*

6 If You See Her, Say Hello (rehearsal)

7 If You See Her, Say Hello—released on *BOTT*

Overdubs: Bob Dylan, mandolin (If You See Her, Say Hello); Chris Weber, twelve-string guitar (If You See Her, Say Hello)

REVIEWS

VARIOUS REVIEWS

New Musical Express (9/18/93)—Ranked #29 in *NME*'s list of the "Greatest Albums of the '70s"

New Musical Express (10/2/93)—Ranked #85 in *NME*'s list of the "Greatest Albums of All Time"

New Musical Express (8/12/00)—Ranked #13 in *NME*'s "Top 30 Heartbreak Albums": ". . . A bitter, sorrowful eulogy to love and the pain of breaking up."

Q magazine (12/93)—(***** rating): ". . . Suddenly Dylan no longer seemed to be straining to recapture the surreal poetic torrents of the '60s. . . . This is probably Dylan's most complete and most unified album—and yes, damnit, his best."

Q magazine (1/03)—Included in *Q*'s "100 Greatest Albums Ever."

Alternative Press (5/01)—Included in *AP*'s "10 Essential Breakup Albums": ". . . Dylan has never been so thematically clear. . . . representing a man full of regret and misery, singing through his tears."

Vibe (12/99)—Included in *Vibe*'s "100 Essential Albums of the 20th Century"

BEST OF LISTS	PLACE
ROLLING STONE (U.S.)—THE 500 GREATEST ALBUMS OF ALL TIME (2003)	16
VILLAGE VOICE (U.S.)—ALBUMS OF THE YEAR	4
NEW MUSICAL EXPRESS (U.K.)—ALBUMS OF THE YEAR	1
SOUNDS (U.K.)—ALBUMS OF THE YEAR	2
OOR (NETHERLANDS)—ALBUMS OF THE YEAR	9
PAUL GAMBACCINI—*THE WORLD CRITICS BEST ALBUMS OF ALL TIME* (1977)	25
ROBERT CHRISTGAU (U.S.)—PERSONAL 40 BEST ALBUMS FROM THE '70S (1979)	26
DAVE MARSH AND KEVIN STEIN (U.S.)—*THE 40 BEST OF ALBUM CHARTMAKERS BY YEAR* (1981)	6
NEW MUSICAL EXPRESS (U.K.)—ALL TIME TOP 100 ALBUMS (1985)	51
PAUL GAMBACCINI—*THE WORLD CRITICS BEST ALBUMS OF ALL TIME* (1987)	25
ROLLING STONE (U.S.)—TOP 100 ALBUMS OF THE LAST 20 YEARS (1987)	12

OOR (NETHERLANDS)—THE BEST ALBUMS OF
THE 20TH CENTURY (1987) 94

HOT PRESS (IRELAND)—THE 100 BEST ALBUMS OF ALL TIME (1989) 2

TIME OUT (U.K.)—THE 100 BEST ALBUMS OF ALL TIME (1989) 33

ROLLING STONE (U.S.)—STEVE POND'S 50 (+27) ESSENTIAL
ALBUMS OF THE 70S (1990) 6

SLITZ (SWEDEN)—THE 50 BEST ALBUMS OF ALL TIME (1990) 40

OOR (NETHERLANDS)—THE BEST ALBUMS OF 1971–1991 (1991) 12

ZOUNDS (GERMANY)—THE TOP 30 ALBUMS OF ALL TIME +
TOP 10 BY DECADE (1992) 11

NEW MUSICAL EXPRESS (U.K.)—ALL TIME TOP 100 ALBUMS +
TOP 50 BY DECADE (1993) 85

MUSIK EXPRESS/SOUNDS (GERMANY)—THE 100 MASTERPIECES (1993) 17

POP (SWEDEN)—THE WORLD'S 100 BEST ALBUMS +
300 COMPLEMENTS (1994) 24

MOJO (U.K.)—THE 100 GREATEST ALBUMS EVER MADE (1995) 39

ADRESSEAVISEN (NORWAY)—THE 100 (+23) BEST
ALBUMS OF ALL TIME (1995) 22

RADIO WXPN (U.S.)—THE 100 MOST PROGRESSIVE ALBUMS (1996) 59

GUARDIAN (U.K.)—THE 100 BEST ALBUMS EVER (1997) 39

ROLLING STONE (GERMANY)—THE BEST ALBUMS OF 5 DECADES (1997) 21

Q (U.K.)—THE 50 BEST ALBUMS OF THE 70S (1998) 15

BERLIN MEDIA (GERMANY)—THE 100 BEST ALBUMS OF ALL TIME (1998) 24

GEAR (U.S.)—THE 100 GREATEST ALBUMS OF THE CENTURY (1999)   44

EXPRESSEN (SWEDEN)—THE 100 BEST RECORDS EVER (1999)   10

PANORAMA (NORWAY)—THE 30 BEST ALBUMS OF
THE YEAR 1970–98 (1999)   2

DAVID KLEIJWEGT (NETHERLANDS)—TOP 100
ALBUMS OF ALL TIME (1999)   52

THE REVIEW, UNIVERSITY OF DELAWARE (U.S.)—100 GREATEST
ALBUMS OF ALL TIME (2001)   32

VH1 (U.S.)—*THE 100 GREATEST ALBUMS OF R 'N' R* (2001)   29

COMPLETE BOOK OF THE BRITISH CHARTS (U.K.)—
JON KUTNER'S TOP 10 ALBUMS (2001)   3

NEW MUSICAL EXPRESS (U.K.)—TOP 100 ALBUMS OF ALL
TIME (2003)   47

POPSTER (ITALY)—THE 100 BEST
ALBUMS OF THE 70S (1979)   NO ORDER

TROUSER (U.S.)—THE BEST ALBUMS
FROM 1970–79 (1980)   NO ORDER

BUSCADERO (ITALY)—THE BEST ALBUMS FROM
THE 1950S TO THE 1980S (1990)   NO ORDER

BILL SHAPIRO (U.S.)—*THE TOP 100 ROCK
COMPACT DISCS* (1991)   NO ORDER

CHUCK EDDY (U.S.)—*THE ACCIDENTAL HISTORY OF
ROCK 'N' ROLL* (1997)   NO ORDER

ROLLING STONE (U.S.)—THE ESSENTIAL 200
ROCK RECORDS (1997)   NO ORDER

LIST BY ASIAN CRITICS—100 ESSENTIAL ALBUMS (1998?)	NO ORDER
VIBE (U.S.)—100 ESSENTIAL ALBUMS OF THE 20TH CENTURY (1999)	NO ORDER
EGGEN AND KARTVEDT (NORWAY)—*THE GUIDE TO THE 100 IMPORTANT ROCK ALBUMS* (1999)	NO ORDER
ROBERT CHRISTGAU (U.S.)—*ROBERT CRISTGAU'S RECORD GUIDE* (1981)	GRADE A
ELVIS COSTELLO—*500 ALBUMS YOU NEED* (2000)	NO ORDER
JIM IRVIN AND PAT GILBERT, EDS. (U.K.)—*THE MOJO COLLECTION: THE ULTIMATE MUSIC COMPANION* (2000)	NO ORDER
NEW MUSICAL EXPRESS (U.K.)—*NME ROCK YEARS*, ALBUMS OF THE YEAR 1963–99 (2000)	NO ORDER
MOJO (U.K.)—*MOJO 1000: THE ULTIMATE CD BUYERS GUIDE* (2001)	NO ORDER
STUART MACONIE'S CRITICAL LIST BBC RADIO 2 (U.K.)— ONE ALBUM ADDED EACH WEEK	NO ORDER
BLENDER (U.S.)—500 CDS YOU MUST OWN BEFORE YOU DIE (2003)	NO ORDER
ROLLING STONE ALBUM GUIDE (U.S.), RATINGS 1–5 STARS (1992)	5 STARS
JOSÉ RAMÓN PARDO (SPAIN)—*THE 1000 BEST POP-ROCK ALBUMS*, RATINGS 1–5 STARS (1997)	4.5 STARS
MUSICHOUND ROCK AND R&B (U.S.)—ALBUM RATINGS 0–5 BONES (1998–99)	5 BONES
PAUL ROLAND (U.K.)—*CD GUIDE TO POP & ROCK*, ALBUM RATINGS 1–5 STARS (2001)	5 STARS

ALL MUSIC GUIDE (U.S.)—ALBUM RATINGS 1–5 STARS (YEAR)   5 STARS

MARTIN C. STRONG (U.K.)—*THE GREAT ROCK DISCOGRAPHY*,
6TH EDITION, RATINGS 1–10 (2002)   10

VIRGIN ENCYCLOPEDIA OF POPULAR MUSIC (U.K.)—
RATINGS 1–5 STARS (2002)   5 STARS

Original recordings and outtakes from the *Blood on the Tracks* sessions have appeared on no less than six Columbia releases and countless bootlegs, with the New York session acetates leading the way for hard-core "boot" collectors. In addition to their official *Blood on the Tracks* vinyl release, plus Half-Speed Mastered vinyl, cassette, CD, MiniDisc, and SACD versions of the album, Columbia's use of the original material recorded for *Blood on the Tracks* includes:

Tangled Up in Blue (1975):

Single (1975): #33 Billboard Charts
Also included as bonus track on Columbia's hybrid SACD soundtrack to *Masked and Anonymous* (2003).

Biograph (1985) includes:

"You're a Big Girl Now" (New York session outtake from 9/25/74)
"Tangled Up in Blue" (New York session outtake from 9/19/74)
"Up to Me" (New York session outtake from 9/25/74)

Bootleg Series, Vols. 1–3 (1991) includes:

"Tangled Up in Blue" (New York session outtake from 9/16/74)
"Call Letter Blues" (New York session outtake from 9/16/74)
"Idiot Wind" (outtake from New York session 9/19/74)

Bob Dylan's Greatest Hits, Vol. 3 (1994) includes:

"Tangled Up in Blue" (official release, from Minneapolis session 12/30/74)—Musicians' names credited (but misspelled!)

The Essential Bob Dylan (2000) includes:

"Tangled Up in Blue" (official release, from Minneapolis session 12/30/74)
"Shelter from the Storm" (official release, from New York session 9/17/74)

To date, *Blood on the Tracks* has sold more than 3 million units, consistently running neck-and-neck with the sales figures of *Desire*, Dylan's other best-selling studio LP. Although Dylan's *Greatest Hits* collections have sold far more in sheer numbers, these are the best-selling studio albums in Bob Dylan's recorded works.

The album's back cover was changed to another painting when Pete Hamill's original liner notes were first excised, then hastily reinstated following a Grammy nomination. Today there are dozens of official versions, jackets, and formats of *Blood on the Tracks* circulating around the world, none of which have accurate credits.

BIBLIOGRAPHY

BOOKS

Baez, Joan. *And a Voice to Sing With*. New York: Summit, 1987.

Dylan, Bob. *Lyrics 1962–1985*. London: Jonathan Cape, 1987.

Engel, Dave. *Just Like Bob Zimmerman's Blues: Dylan in Minnesota*. Rudolph, WI: River City Memoirs Mesabi, 1997.

Gambaccini, Paul. *Critics' Choice: Top 100 Albums of All Time*. New York: Harmony Books, 1987.

Gill, Andy. *My Back Pages: Classic Bob Dylan 1962–1969*. London: Carlton Books, 1998.

Gray, Michael. *Song and Dance Man III: The Art of Bob Dylan*. London: Cassell, 2000.

Gray, Michael, and Bauldie, John (eds.). *All Across the Telegraph: A Bob Dylan Handbook*. London: Sidgwick & Jackson, 1987.

Hajdu, David. *Positively 4th Street*. New York: Farrar, Straus & Giroux, 2001.

Heylin, Clinton. *Bob Dylan: The Recording Sessions 1960–1994*. New York: St. Martin's Press, 1995.

Heylin, Clinton. *Behind the Shades Revisited: The Bob Dylan Biography*. New York: William Morrow, 2001.

Klagsbrun, Francine. *Mixed Feelings: Love, Hate, Rivalry and Reconciliation Among Brothers and Sisters*. New York: Bantam, 1992.

McDonough, Jimmy. *Shakey: Neil Young's Biography*. New York: Random House, 2002.

Plaut, W. Gunther (ed.). *The Torah: A Modern Commentary*. New York: Union of Hebrew Congregations, 1981.

Riley, Tim. *Hard Rain: A Dylan Commentary*. New York: Da Capo, 1999.

Shelton, Robert. *No Direction Home: The Life and Music of Bob Dylan*. New York: Da Capo, 1997.

Shepard, Sam. *The Rolling Thunder Logbook*. New York: Penguin, 1977.

Sloman, Larry. *On the Road with Bob Dylan*. New York: Three Rivers Press/Random House, 2002.

Sounes, Howard. *Down the Highway: The Life of Bob Dylan*. New York: Grove Press, 2001.

Spitz, Bob. *Dylan: A Biography*. New York: McGraw-Hill, 1989.

Thompson, Toby. *Positively Main Street*. New York: Warner Books, 1972.

Thomson, Elizabeth, and Gutman, David (eds.). *The Dylan Companion*. London: Macmillan, 1990.

Williams, Paul. *Bob Dylan: Performing Artist, The Middle Years 1974–1986*. Lancaster, PA: Underwood-Miller, 1992.

Williams, Paul. *Bob Dylan: Watching the River Flow—Observations on His Art in Progress 1966–1995*. London: Omnibus Press, 1996.

Zollo, Paul. *Songwriters on Songwriting*. New York: Da Capo, 2003.

PERIODICALS

Bay, Monica. Title unknown. *Minnesota Daily*, January 10, 1975.

Bream, Jon. "Tangled Up in Retakes." *Creem*, Vol. 6, No. 11, 1975.

Cartwright, Bert. "Dylan's Mysterious Man Called Norman." *The Telegraph*, Vol. 23, 1986.

Cartwright, Bert. "Dylan's Mysterious Man Called Norman Raeben." *The Telegraph*, Vol. 26, 1987.

Cowan, Paul. "Bob Dylan: *Blood on the Tracks*." *Village Voice*, February 3, 1975.

Cusimano, Jim. "Dylan Comes Back to the Wars." *Crawdaddy*, April 1975.

Editors of *Rolling Stone*. "The Best Albums of the Last Twenty Years." *Rolling Stone*, Vol. 507, August 27, 1987.

Gill, Andy. "So Much Older Then . . . : The Making of Blood on the Tracks." *Mojo*, Vol. 91, June 2001.

Goldwasser, Noe. "Do What You Must Do and Do It Well." *Rock*, March 1975.

Harris, John. "Why Does It Always Rain on Me?" *Q Dylan Special*, October 2000.

Kot, Greg. "100 Greatest Pop Songs." *Rolling Stone*, Vol. 855, December 21, 2000.

Landau, John. "Blood on the Tracks: After the Flood." *Rolling Stone*, Vol. 182, March 13, 1975.

Metsa, Paul, and Mischke, Tom. "An Interview with Kevin Odegard." *On the Tracks,* Vol. 21, 2001.

Nelson, Paul. "Top Critics Track Dylan." *Rolling Stone,* Vol. 182, March 13, 1975.

Odegard, Kevin. "Tangled Up in Bob." *MPLS ST. PAUL Magazine,* March, 2001.

"Random Notes." *Rolling Stone,* Vol. 181, February 13, 1975.

Scoppa, Bud. "Top Critics Track Dylan." *Rolling Stone,* Vol. 182, March 13, 1975.

Walsh, Jim. "Dylan Came to Minnesota to Paint His Masterpiece." *St. Paul Pioneer Press,* 2001.

Zollo, Paul. "The Bob Dylan Interview." *Songtalk,* 1991.

"Bob Dylan: *Blood on the Tracks*." *Time,* February 17, 1975.

SPECIAL THANKS

The authors offer special thanks to each of the following persons, without whom this project could not have been completed. Your help is sincerely and deeply appreciated.

KEN ABDO

BRIAN E. ANDERSON

AL ARONOWITZ

BRIAN BALOGH

CLINTON BEECHAM

PETE BENNION

BILL BERG

JAMES BERTRAM

RICH BETTIS

STEPHEN M. H. BRAITMAN

RICHARD BRAUN

JON BREAM

PAUL BRESNICK

CHARLIE BROWN III

PETER STONE BROWN

TONY BROWN

NANCY BUNDT

BUDDY CAGE

ROB CHAPPELL

BURTON COHEN

RICHARD CROOKS

TONI AND RON DACHIS

GARY DIAMOND

LAMONT DOZIER

BARBARA DUFFY

MARK ELLEN

DAVE ENGEL

RICHARD FINE

IDY GARVIS

PAT GILBERT

LINDA GILL

BARBARA GLASER

RABBI SIM GLASER

DANNY GOLDBERG

ELIZABETH GORZELANY

PAUL GREIN

DAVID HAJDU

KEVIN HANOVER

JOHN HARRIS

JOHN HENKEL

JAMES HESSELGRAVE

CLINTON HEYLIN

T. DAN HOFSTEDT

DEBORAH HOPP

GREGG INHOFER

FRED AND RHEA ISAACS

JEFF JOHNSON

JOHN JOHNSON

KATE KAZENIAC

JEFF KLEPPER

AL KOOPER

GREG KOT

MICHAEL KROGSGAARD

FRED KROHN

RANDY LEVY

GARY LOPAC

GREIL MARCUS

PAUL MARTINSON

JOHN MCANDREW

MICK AND LAURIE MCCUISTION

TOM MCFAUL

PAUL METSA, SONGWRITER AND ACTIVIST

TOMMY MORGAN

BARBARA PERKINS ODEGARD

JENNY, JESSIE, AND MINDY ODEGARD

LINDA CARLSON ODEGARD

ROBERT J. ODEGARD

STEPHEN JAMES ODEGARD

ON THE TRACKS MAGAZINE

CHARLIE AND CAROL OSSELL

PETER OSTROUSHKO

BILL PAGEL

D. A. PENNEBAKER

BILLY PETERSON

CHRISTINE PRICE

JOHN RADZIEWICZ

PHIL RAMONE

DAVID RIVKIN

MARION RIVMAN

ROBBIE ROBERTSON

HILARY ROSEN

LEON RUSSELL

MARLY RUSOFF

ROWLAND SALLEY

BEN SCHAFER

KEVIN SCHIEFFER

SAM SIEDEN

BARBARA SLAVIN

LARRY SLOMAN

BOB SPITZ

ERIN SPRAGUE

JOE STANGER

ELLEN STEINMAN

DAVID STEVENS

WILLIAM SWANSON

ERIC THIRY

PHYLLIS AND BRUCE THOMPSON

TOBY THOMPSON

ARTIE TRAUM

HAPPY TRAUM

PAUL TRYNKA

BILL WANNER

CHRIS AND VANESSA WEBER

ERIC WEISSBERG

JANN WENNER

TOM WHELAN

WENDY WHETSELL

PAUL WILLIAMS

SUSAN O. WOOD

NANCY O. YOUNGMAN

DAVID Z

SUE AND AL ZELICKSON

CHARLIE ZELLE

DAVID ZIMMERMAN

PAUL ZOLLO

INDEX